MW01105780

THE
AUDACITY
OF FAITH

SAM BELONY

RealityCheck
PUBLISHING

Superman has his body of steel and laser vision.
Batman has his gadgets and the Batmobile.
Bees have their sting and dogs have their bark;
I have you: you're my secret weapon!

I dedicate this book to Nahum Sissan Belony,
my Mrs. Babes. Your love, support and drive
motivate and inspire me to strive for excellence.
You'll always be my favoritest!

CONTENTS

STAGE FOUR: CULMINATION

ACKNOWLEDGEMENTS

PEOPLE TEND TO credit authors for the success of books, not realizing that, just as it takes a village to raise a child, it takes an army to publish a book. I am grateful to those whose love and influences brought this book to fruition. I am especially indebted to:

Grace Brown, for your straightforwardness and critical eye.

Grace Virtue, for your thoughtful insights and, especially, your patience.

My very good friend, Dr. Farly Sejour, for your enthusiasm, encouragement, and support.

My mother, Simone Aurelien: Your love is rock solid; I am grateful to God for your presence in my life. Everything I am, every opportunity I have, is thanks to you. I love you!

My little brother, Sadrack "Shad" Belony, who inspires me to be a better man.

My sister, Carline Charles: You live your faith every day. I would not be a Christian today if not for you.

Lastly, my queen, my partner, my first editor, and after Jesus, my anchor: Nahum. You exemplify the meaning of your name, comfort in distress. I love you more than I can say.

O

THE GREATEST FIVE-LETTER WORD

MY WIFE AND I have many things in common, but our shopping habits are not among them.

When I need something at the store I run straight to the aisle, grab what I want, pay the cashier, and get out of there as fast as I can!

Not my wife.

Nahum usually browses the aisles from one end of the store to the other. She compares prices and brands to get the best deals and maximize the value of her trip. The only time I shop like my wife is when I go to brick and mortar bookstores.

My love affair with bookstores stems from my love of words. Because I love words, I often wondered what is considered the greatest word in the English language.

A quick Google search returned a few "best words" lists that included favorites like love and serendipity and lesser-known words such as dicephalous, clishmaclaver, and facetious. However, I found no evidence of anyone trying to identify the one word that rules all others. While working on this book I decided to at least identify what I believe to be the greatest of five-letter words. Consider some of the most common contenders:

Death is the universal destroyer of life. It terrorizes man the moment he becomes conscious of the world. Death shows no mercy for the weak, no prejudice toward the wealthy. It is an enemy that can also be a friend, ending the pain of the sufferer while guaranteeing the demise of the criminal or terrorist. Death is a most fearful and intriguing word.

Grace is imperial. It emanates grandeur and elegance, and stands for everything that is refined and charming. Above all, salvation is not possible without it; God's greatest gift to mankind came through the conduit of grace. Grace is, indeed, a fascinating word!

Truth is another great word, but one that has unfortunately become the victim of modern thinking. The idea of objective, absolute truth has become as rotten as old meat. Today's mind prefers relative truth—truth that tickles the ears and placates tensions, truth that is cuddly and touchy-feely, truth that does not offend. But without *true* truth we would have a most difficult time navigating our way through life, for the One who is Truth is also Life (John 14:6). Truth is an indispensable word.

Who can ignore the influence of words like mercy, power, peace, greed, and money? The majesty of royal, noble and crown? The worthiness of honor, glory and might? The grumpiness of fraud, nasty, rogue and rowdy? And the virulence of pride and Satan?

Nevertheless, in my mind, none of these words deserve the scepter to rule other words. The one word that I would coronate as the greatest of five-letter words is: *FAITH!*

Faith is absolutely indispensable to our existence; it is the single most important currency in the universe. We need faith to navigate life, and we express it when we eat, drive our cars, board an airplane, or buy a dress. When it comes to salvation, no weapon in our Christian arsenal is as powerful or effective.

God's power is ours by faith. It is through faith that we receive grace and abide by God's truth, even when it is difficult, offensive, and its demands go against our better judgment. Faith leads us to risk our livelihood, our relationships, and our very lives for the sake of the gospel.

Jesus, the name above every name, through whom God made and sustains the world, is accessed only by faith. His divinity, humanity, and ministry in heaven on our behalf are accepted by faith. Heaven's greatest treasure—the good news of salvation, the gospel of truth—is foolishness to us unless we accept and obey it by faith. Without it, we cannot attain God's pure standard of righteousness.

Faith is truly the greatest five-letter word.

FAITH IS THE SECRET TO PLEASING GOD

THIS book progresses in four stages. In stage one, *Infancy,* we explore the nature of faith, what it is, how it relates to life, and the role of miracles. When we reach stage two, *Maturity,* we see how God begins to grow our faith. Using the chisel of affliction, He chips away the defects in our characters and transforms us into usable tools in His hands.

Intimacy, the third stage, brings us to new heights in our relationship with God. The assignments get tougher at this stage, but by then we've been around the block with Him a few times, and have learned that He can be trusted. We also learn about His expectations of us, about our responsibilities toward Him and toward our fellowmen.

The last stage, *Culmination,* is probably the reason why most people join the Christian faith: the reward—God's blessings, His daily provisions, and above all, eternal life. But at this stage we learn that Christianity is much more than this. It is also about what we become as a result of having faith—how we respond to God's apparent neglect or abandonment. Culmination focuses on our response to faith after we have become intimate with its Author and Finisher, on how we view this life from the vantage point of eternity.

My attempt in writing this book is not to encapsulate faith in God with a set of principles and how-to's. Instead I hope to share my experiences with faith. I am by no means an "expert" on faith; the Lord only knows how little I knew when I began this project and how much I still have to learn. But too many authors and ministers present watered-down, black market versions of faith. I hope to refute those ersatz versions and present the *true* faith of the Bible: the faith that is utterly rewarding but that has been forged in the crucible of affliction; the faith that strengthens us in the face of insurmountable odds, that imbues us with a defiant boldness to confidently face life's hardest challenges. Above all, I want to present the faith that transforms, that indelibly imprints upon us the character of Jesus Christ. It is the secret to pleasing God.

INFANCY

Faith Is the Currency of Life

I

THE POWER TO SWING GOD'S ARMS

THE EARTH, SCIENTISTS tell us, spins 360 degrees on its axis during a 24-hour period at a speed of roughly 1,000 miles per hour. It plows through space in its yearly orbit around the sun at a face-flattening speed of 67,000 miles per hour. The sun itself is moving, blasting around the center of our galaxy at a mind-numbing velocity of 560,000 miles per hour!

Scientists also explain that the earth's rotation on its axis toward the east is what controls sunrise and sunset. Your location experiences daylight each time the earth completes a 24-hour cycle and the sun comes back into view.

I really wanted to know what would happen should the earth suddenly stop its rotation. What calamity would befall us earthlings—busy with our impressive jobs, dinner reservations, and family trips—if for some reason the earth, which heretofore has managed to faithfully perform its duties, decided one day to simply quit, walk out on the job? I turned to science for help, and came up with a multitude of answers.

Some scientists believe that conservation of momentum would keep us spinning and send us jetting toward the east at bone-crushing speeds.

Some believe that the oceans would unleash their fury against us, washing the earth's surfaces with giant tidal waves.

Some say nothing would happen; we would stay put, but continual darkness on one side of the earth and continual sunlight on the other would result in its own form of calamity.

Buildings would crumble. There would be large atmospheric winds at the earth's surfaces, massive earthquakes, and fireballs that would consume everything in their path!

"The earth would split in half" others add. And on and on the list of ensuing devastating disasters goes.

Although the scientists differ in what they believe might happen, they all seem to agree on one thing: a halt in the earth's rotation is impossible. "Of course, this can't happen" one astrophysicist said. "This scenario can't really happen," another expert concurred. They have the laboratory reports and data-validated analyses to back up their claims.

An object in motion will remain in motion unless acted upon by an outside force, they insist. This means that for the earth to somehow stop its rotation there would have to be "an impactor"—an object strong enough to cross its path and cause the halt. Science assures us that there are no such objects in our solar system; any objects in our universe that might have otherwise been a threat are positioned so that they can never collide with the earth in such a manner.

But the Bible says there was a day—"there has never been a day like it before or since"—when the sun did the unthinkable. Joshua, Israel's intrepid leader after the death of Moses, had the audacity to pray, and in response the sun stopped dead in the middle of the skies and did not set for an entire extra day (Joshua 10:12–14).

We are not given the details on how this happened—there is no scientific data, no laboratory analysis to help us construct a blueprint or explain the mysteries behind that dramatic occurrence. Since the earth's rotation is what controls "sunrise" and "sunset," did Joshua's prayer bring the earth to a screeching halt? What's remarkable is that there was no earthquake or tidal waves, and no human, car, or cow was flung off the surface of the earth at speeds twice that of sound.

It was not a massive "impactor" that struck the earth to prevent the sun from setting. The sun stayed put simply in obedience to the prayer of a former slave!

FAITH IS THE CURRENCY OF LIFE

IMAGINE a person who goes through life with absolutely no faith.

She manages to lead an incredible faithless existence trusting no one and believing in nothing. She does her own hair because she has no faith in hairstylists, makes her own toothbrushes and toothpastes, and digs her own well to find potable water. She does not wear deodorant or perfume, and does not consult with doctors because she does not believe in their ability to treat her. She does not believe in engineers, so the faithless one would not cross bridges, drive cars, or, heaven forbid, fly in airplanes. Trust her politicians? Forget it—she runs her own country and obeys her own laws.

This is all sounding unreasonable to you, isn't it? That's because it is.

Everyone exercises faith in one form or another. Because you have reasonable confidence in your barber's sanity and competence, you sit in his chair despite the sharp pair of scissors in his hands and trust him not to stab you or botch your hair with them. You trust in the engineers' knowledge and due diligence, so you agree to climb aboard the crazy machine at the local amusement park for an adrenaline-pumping thrill ride, allowing the thing to fling you left and right, twist you up and down, and shake you until your insides threaten to fly out through your nose. You scream like a child, yet are ecstatic, even as the thing drops you 200 feet from the air.

If this isn't faith, then I don't know what is.

Every creature on planet earth that has a heart operates by faith. Just as nations exchange their own currencies, human beings use faith naturally and effortlessly in all of our exchanges. Faith, in this sense, is what we commonly refer to as *trust*.

Merriam-Webster defines trust as "assured reliance on the character, ability, strength, or truth of something or someone." You trust your surgeon to such a degree that you lie unconscious on his operating table and allow that total stranger to cut you open, insert tubes into your heart and bypass it with a cardiopulmonary machine while he works on it to repair a valve. In some cases he discards your heart altogether and puts someone else's heart back into your chest.

Trusting him with your life is not a sign that you've gone mad and should be confined to an insane asylum, but proof that the advancements in medicine have greatly improved our lives, and in turn gives you great confidence. You engage in this expensive, dangerous procedure because you *hope* it will yield dividends in the form of a better quality of life.

Many define faith as belief or conviction in something "for which there is no proof." They argue that faith is opposed to reason, as if it requires the deactivation of our brains and the uninstallation of sanity. But that is not faith. While it is true that faith buoys us beyond the dangers of doubt to experience the unseen and the not yet—i.e., a better life with a new heart—it does not require us to completely ignore logic or to naively accept the irrational in spite of strong evidence to the contrary. While it transcends proof, faith is neither blind nor foolish.

The faith we have in our surgeon is analogous to the biblical faith, except on a grander scale.

We decide at some point that God may actually know what He

is talking about. If He could pull off the biblical six-day creation and make this amazing body that we possess, then perhaps He may have some skills that could be of value to us. So, impressed with His prowess, we start by obeying the command to follow Him for selfish reasons, much like we trust our doctors because of what we believe they can do for us.

But the faith that started with a relatively small decision to obey over time develops into something greater. Through obedience we learn fundamental truths about God. It becomes obvious that He can be trusted, so we give Him more credit. As we trust Him, He proves Himself loving, gracious, compassionate, and slow to anger. He proves Himself worthy of more trust, worthy of our complete surrender and unreserved loyalty.

As we delve deeper into the vast ocean of His love we begin to wonder how a God so awesome, so limitless in power and glory can love such puny creatures as ourselves. The moment we think we've reached the crest of His delight, we discover that we had not even scratched the surface.

By then our hearts are so intertwined with God's heart that no matter what He commands, we will obey in a heartbeat. This is where we reach the Hebrews 11 faith—the faith that is the currency of life; the faith that needs no physical evidence to believe the impossible, trust the incredible and the mind-blowing, and tolerate the intolerable simply because God says so.

It is not that there can be no proof or that reason does not apply; it is simply that the relationship has reached a level that transcends proof to tap into the very character of God, a level of knowing Him that takes us beyond anything our eyes can see or our minds understand, a degree of alignment of our wills with His, a tuning of our hearts to the frequencies of His heart, that far surpasses the acuteness of our senses.

"Faith means striking out, with no clear end in sight and perhaps even no clear view of the next step. It means following, trusting, holding out a hand to an invisible Guide....Faith is reason gone courageous—not the opposite of reason, to be sure, but something more than reason and never satisfied by reason alone."[1]

FAITH IS THE EVIDENCE

SOME of us still want proof! We want God to burst onto the scene and show Himself.

Flex Your almighty muscles, Lord! Let me see that Mr. Universe body of Yours. Show me those arms that are supposedly so strong they carry all of humanity. Open those large palms that have got the whole world in them. Show me Your strength—give me a glimpse of Your awesomeness, just a glimpse of Your remarkableness, Your breathtaking, awe-inspiring, splendiferous presence! I want to see You for myself. We want dramatic, earth-shattering evidence that God is out there somewhere.

And what do we get in response? Dead silence. At best, mere whispers. God stays hidden behind the curtains. He refuses to show Himself, to answer questions. The worse our situations get, it seems, the more God remains hidden, and the more deafening His silence. God has a purpose for His deliberate concealment, and that purpose is, among other things, to grow our faith.

Substance Faith

The Bible defines faith as "the substance of things hoped for" (Hebrews 11:1, NKJV). To put it differently, faith is the essential nature, the ultimate reality, the materialization of our hope. Faith takes what we anticipate from God, reaches beyond our dimension into the realms of eternal grace, marries it with the power of the Almighty, and makes it a reality. Faith in God takes hope and gives it matter—it gives *substance* to our hope.

Substance faith anchors our hearts to God. It imbues us with a passion for God, a passion for His Word, for His glory, and for the honor of His name. We no longer serve God because of the "stuff" that He gives us. As pastor and author Craig Groeschel puts it, God is no longer to us "a cosmic sugar daddy."[2] Faith becomes about a Person. The fact that He is the all-knowing, all-powerful God who assembled and animated a block of dirt and from it brought forth the intelligent beings we turn out to be, puts Him in a position where He is entitled to our total trust. Substance faith brings intimacy, and closeness, and love. When it powers our lives, we move by the promptings of God's Spirit, not by what we see or hear (see 2 Corinthians 5:7).

This kind of faith is so daring it is downright dangerous. It counts its chickens before they are hatched. In fact, it meets with clients, strikes up deals, and makes a profit on those chickens. Some wonders whether such a faith is presumption. The answer is an emphatic "No!" That is because this faith is not based on feelings or presuppositions, but on the unshakable, immovable, holding-the-universe-together Word of God.

And God expects this kind of faith. He expected it from Daniel facing an angry King Nebuchadnezzar. He expected it from ninety-nine-year-old Abraham and his ninety-year-old wife Sarah, who laughed at the thought of birthing a child at their ripe age. And He expects it from you and me. "'Whatever you ask for in prayer,'" Jesus said to Peter's amazement at the withered fig tree, "'believe that *you have received it*, and it will be yours'" (Mark 11:24).

Some consider such faith imprudent or illogical, but the measure of your faith will determine your degree of experience with God. The more faith you have—the more daring and mettlesome—the greater the opportunity to see God move wonderfully in your life. "When Jesus saw their faith, he said to the paralytic...." (Mark 2:5). "Jesus turned and saw her. 'Take heart, daughter,' he said, 'your faith has healed you'" (Matthew 9:22). "'According to your faith will it be done to you'" Christ told the blind man (verse 29). "And he did not do many miracles there because of their lack of faith" (13:58).

I must admit that I do not yet have the kind of substance faith that many of the bold Bible patriarchs are famous for. My faith has never parted oceans or made manna rain from heaven or raised the dead or shut the mouths of angry lions. I struggle with the faith that heals minor sicknesses or puts up with difficulties. What gives me hope is a pattern that I see in the Gospels.

I am comforted when I realize that Jesus never turned anyone away who came to Him in faith. Whether the person had the marvelously great faith of the Canaanite woman (Matthew 15:21–28) or the meager trust of the father who amazed Jesus when he said, "'*If you can do anything*, take pity on us and help us'" (Mark 9:22), God stooped down to honor their faith.

Still, I desire the great faith that stiffens my spine and gives me audacity. I desire the faith that lives and breathes to honor God, the faith that becomes a bridge over the sea of impossibility, that is assurance in times of disaster, and the realization of my hopes and dreams. I desire the faith that aligns my plans with God's.

I want faith to become the substance of my life!

Proof of the Pudding

The idiom that many people know today as, "The proof is in the pudding" is actually a short, misquoted version of the original phrase: "The proof of the pudding is in the eating," which dates back to the 14th century. The phrase's actual meaning is: The only way to test the quality or truth of something is to experience it for yourself.

The author of Hebrews writes, "Faith is the...evidence of things not seen" (Hebrews 11:1, NKJV). Faith serves as the confirmation, the authenticating factor of the reality of those things that we cannot see. It is a settled assurance, an established confidence that those things exist because, although they are not seen, they can be *lived*.

I have never seen air. I don't fully understand how my lungs work—how breathing is used to release energy, improve blood flow, or remove carbon dioxide from my body. But I know that I am alive because I am able to breathe freely, and feel the air moving in and out of my lungs. Those facts serve as enough evidence to me that air exists.

The proof of faith is grounded in a *Person*. Because of my relationship with God and my confidence in Him, when He makes a promise, I need no further proof that it will find its fulfillment in due time. As a result, I am able to enjoy today what is promised to be mine tomorrow, next year, in ten years, or when Christ returns.* My hope finds substance and becomes a living reality I can take possession of now. I need no outside claims to corroborate my faith— no mathematical models or expert testimonials to serve as objective evidence. The evidence I need I find in the Person whom I trust, in the irrevocability of His word. Faith in Him serves as my final proof.

You will find that most people who deny God's existence don't know anything about Him. They draw conclusions based on presuppositions grounded in what they don't know—not what they know. They deny creation without knowing the Creator, reject the notion of miracles without understanding the mind and heart of the One who performs such miracles.

Once you've been acquainted with Christ and have slackened your thirsty throat by imbibing from the refreshing oasis of His love, once you've shared His company and have gotten to know Him for

---

* When I get an offer for a new job, I do not wait to actually start with the new company before I consider myself employed by it. I go out and celebrate with loved ones before I start the job; I update my budget to reflect the new salary, and begin to think in terms of the new position and how it will impact my life. Faith in God's promises should be lived the moment we are confident our prayer is heard and our petitions are granted.

yourself, once your relationship with Him is no longer based on what your preacher said or your nana believed or the newscaster reported or the scientist explained, then you cannot help but to utterly trust Him.

Accepting the fact that God created matter by calling it into existence is only inconceivable if I don't know God. "God saw all that he had made, and it was very good. And there was evening, and there was morning—the sixth day" (Genesis 1:31). When I personally know God, Genesis 1 is all I need to believe that He did in fact create the universe in six literal 24-hour days. I don't need someone to travel back in time with a video recorder and bring back footage; I don't need a journalist at the scene of Creation to interview God and later present me with an eyewitness account; and I don't need to go witness Creation for myself. God's Word is evidence enough that what He says is true. Anything beyond that is flagrant disregard for His Person and nullifies faith.

THE POWER TO SWING GOD'S ARMS

HEZEKIAH was one of Judah's best kings. A far cry from his wicked and reckless father, Ahaz, Hezekiah was both a prosperous king and a strong spiritual leader. He repaired and cleansed the temple, destroyed the idols and the high places, celebrated a grandiose Passover with the ten Tribes of the Northern Kingdom of Israel, and had Solomon's unpublished proverbs recorded. Militarily Hezekiah defeated the Philistines and through faith in God saw the destruction of Sennacherib's powerful Assyrian army. In addition to spiritual and military successes, Hezekiah was also very wealthy.

"Hezekiah had very great riches and honor, and he made treasuries for his silver and gold and for his precious stones, spices, shields and all kinds of valuables. He also made buildings to store the harvest of grain, new wine and oil; and he made stalls for various kinds of cattle, and pens for the flocks. He built villages and acquired great numbers of flocks and herds, for God had given him very great riches" (2 Chronicles 32:27-29).

But fourteen years into his powerful reign, this great king was struck with a deadly disease (2 Kings 20:7). The progression of the disease had reached a critical point, and death was the natural outcome. As the king clung to life, God's prophet Isaiah burst into his bedchamber and shattered his world with the pronouncement of his doom: *Your Majesty, God says, "Make your final arrangements: you're going to die!"* (Isaiah 38:1, paraphrased).

When he heard the death sentence, Hezekiah "broke down and wept bitterly" (Isaiah 38:3, NLT). Desperate, down and out, the king did not sink into despair or cry *Woe is me!* Instead he petitioned to God, knowing that prayer often leads God to do what He otherwise might not. And God heard and moved upon his words.

"Before Isaiah had left the middle court, the word of the Lord came to him: 'Go back and tell Hezekiah, the leader of my people, "This is what the Lord, the God of your father David, says: I have heard your prayer and seen your tears; I will heal you.... I will add fifteen years to your life" '" (2 Kings 20:4-6).

Shifting God into Gear

The notion is daring, borderline heretical.

This is the God whose presence is a consuming fire, who inspires smoke and thunder and whirlwind; who declares that to see Him in His glorious form is to die. The idea that mere human beings with flesh and bones—fine dust on the surface of a tiny speck of a decaying planet—can move Him seems sacrilegious.

Yet when you read the Bible you will find that human beings just like you and me have done this very thing. We drop down to our shaky, weak human knees, utter a few words of faith, and the great God of heaven moves. We speak here on earth, and at the Central Command Control of the universe—the very throne of God beyond the stars—orders are given and things in the universe get reorganized. Death turns to life. Disease turns to healing. Accidents are avoided. Defeat turns into victory.

The funny thing is, sometimes when we pray, we have no idea what we're talking about. We *think* we know, *act* like we understand, but the reality is that God's Spirit, in His grace, interprets the confounding mess we send His way into something coherent that He then grants according to His own plans for our lives.

God Fills in the Blanks

Joshua thought he knew what he was talking about.

The military general found himself in a complicated mess. The Gibeonites successfully secured a peace treaty with Joshua and the Israelites during their conquest of Canaan by resorting to fraud (see Joshua 9). Pretending to be emissaries of a far country, their representatives claimed to have come to make a pact with this powerful Israelite nation since they had heard "'of the fame of the Lord your God'" (Joshua 9:10). Drinking the tale like fresh water on a hot summer day, the Israelites signed a treaty with the imposters without further investigation, only to learn later that the Gibeonites were actually locals—a neighboring tetrapolis (a four-city confederation) trying to escape the fury of this fighting machine.[3]

When neighboring Canaanite leaders learned of Gibeon's defection, they garnered their forces together and marched against it. Led by Adoni-Zedek, king of Jerusalem, the five-state confederacy descended upon Gibeon like a flood. The Gibeonites sent messengers to Joshua asking for help. Rather than leaving them to reap the rewards of their evil deeds and be destroyed by the five southern nations, Joshua decided to provide military assistance.

Joshua marshaled his troops and began an all-night trek from his camp in Gilgal, which was twenty-five miles from Gibeon, and fell upon the unsuspecting enemies in a surprise early-morning attack.

Unprepared for the battle, which probably followed a night of "revelry and dissipation,"[4] the enemy tried to flee from the Israelite forces, "hoping to reach the fortified cities from which they had set out, seal the gates, and gain at least a night's respite before they had to face their pursuing foes again."[5] God intervened, hurling giant hailstones down on them, eventually causing more deaths with the hailstones than with the swords of Israelite soldiers.

As the battle waged on Joshua realized something: "This was an unprecedented opportunity to destroy the southern confederacy. The best of their soldiers had come out against him, and they were fleeing. If he could destroy them now, the southlands would be open to his advancing armies."[6] At the same time he also realized that half of the day was gone, and the sun would soon set. In those days military activities ended at sundown. If Joshua failed to achieve total victory that day and allowed those soldiers to regroup and attack the next day, he would have a much fiercer fight on his hands, one that would require greater efforts and possible casualties from his side to secure victory. So he got a crazy idea, the craziest any military personnel has ever had.

Deciding that more time was needed to bring about complete victory, the former slave reasoned he would talk the sun into giving him an extra day! "'Let the sun stand still over Gibeon, and the moon over the valley of Aijalon!'" Joshua said (Joshua 10:12, NLT).

This is what I call *out-of-your-mind-crazy* faith!

Here is a man in the midst of a heated battle—swords clanging, spears and arrows flying, hailstones raining from heaven, men falling dead all around him, enemies rushing for cover. Loud battle cries. Agonizing shrieks from the wounded. Chaos everywhere. Amid the bedlam, without thinking about the possible corollaries of his bold command, without so much as a thought of the extent to which his prayer could throw nature into disarray, Joshua simply ordered the sun around.

I found Joshua's action outrageous for a number of reasons.

First, we're talking about the sun here. *The sun!* It's not a soldier, not a donkey or horse or warplane or even military tank—it's a star. A very big, bad, filled-with-gases, 860,000-mile wide star. Its weight in pounds? 4.4 followed by thirty zeros—I don't even know what to call that number! Somebody said it would take about a year and a half to drive across the sun. And, did I mention it is hot? Its core temperature is twenty-seven million degrees Fahrenheit!*

Second, the sun is ninety-three million miles away from earth. It's not our next-door, next-country, or even next-planet neighbor. It's a massive fireball that sits somewhere in the distant sky.

Third, as we know today, the sun does not control daylight; that's actually a function of the earth's rotation on its own axis. If you really wanted to get some extra light you would give your order to the earth. But that's not what happened. Joshua spoke to the sun, and interestingly enough, the record shows that the sun obeyed, like any Israelite soldier would.

We can never know for sure what was going through Joshua's mind during that awesome battle of Gibeon, but we can be certain that he was not worried about the *how* of his command.

Joshua was a former slave, not a scientist. Whether or not he knew about the earth's orbit around the sun or the phenomenon of sunrise and sunset, at that moment he did not seem to care about it. The probable consequences of his bold declaration never crossed his mind. By faith—power-grabbing, nature-halting, move-God's-arm faith—he simply addressed the sun as we would our children, and as any obedient child would, *something* (earth, sun, whatever) obeyed. Equally important, no disaster ensued.

---

* By the way, I am fully aware that, as human beings, we really do not know the actual size, weight, or composition of the sun. We haven't even gotten it right about the origin of life on earth, so take these figures with a grain of salt. I am using them purely for illustrative purposes.

I sense that what made the difference in this instance came from the early part of verse 12. It says Joshua spoke *"to the Lord"* (NKJV), that is, he spoke in the presence *of* the Lord. It was a prayer to God, although he was addressing the sun.

When exercising faith, we don't always need to understand the details of what we are asking. We don't need to be wise like Solomon, eloquent like Elijah, or on fire like John the Baptist. We only need to come to God with a sincere heart, speak our needs "to the Lord," in the presence of the God of heaven, and His Spirit will fill in the blanks for us. He will interpret our hearts' desires even when our vocabularies, our lack of knowledge, and our intellectual limitations prevent us from using the right words. Heaven will listen even when our words don't make much sense.

"The Spirit helps us in our weakness" Paul tells the Romans. "We do not know what we ought to pray for, but the Spirit himself intercedes for us with groans that words cannot express. And he who searches our hearts knows the mind of the Spirit, because the Spirit intercedes for the saints in accordance with God's will" (Romans 8:26, 27).

What Really Happened that Day?

The skeptics have a field day with this Joshua 10 passage. Even religious scholars and commentators struggle to explain what happened. Many suggest alternatives. God used refraction of light to lengthen the day, they say. Some believe these are just words, nothing for us to take literally; to Joshua and the soldiers, it only *felt* as if it had been an additional day. And on and on they go. My question is: What kind of God are they serving that He cannot control His own creation? Why not an earth-stopping miracle—literally?

I think the problem is that too many of us are content with wussy faith. We settle for the retired faith that just wants to lie on the beach and watch the sunset, the lazy couch potato faith that

15

simply sits around while the rest of the world passes by. No wonder our little god sits powerlessly as we struggle all alone with our predicaments, unable to do anything to help.

I must admit that I have absolutely no idea what happened that day. I couldn't tell you what God did or how He did it. What I write about the behavior of the earth and sun, I gathered from reading what science tells me. I have nothing to offer as an alternative, and I am quite content with that because I have no problem accepting the raw miracle of the earth coming to a screeching halt, suddenly, completely, with absolutely no impact on the rest of the universe.

Why? Because I serve a God who can do all things. Does that mean God actually did stop the earth? Not necessarily. After all, He *is* God. He could have used any means He pleased. I simply wish to caution against the urge to rationalize away God's work, to dilute it to the level of our limited conceptions. If God is great enough to speak the world into existence, wise enough to hold it together, He is also powerful enough to stop the earth with no disastrous outcome.

To pray Joshua's prayer, have nature respond to us as she did to him, and move God's arms as powerfully as he did, we need the audacity of faith. We need a faith big enough to rise beyond our own expectations, and grand enough to exceed our limitations. We need the intrepid, blatantly defiant faith of Joshua—the kind of faith that interrupts the natural flow of the world.

LAST WORDS
Prayer Works

FROM MY JOURNAL: JULY 2006

I was on my way home from work when the transmission on my fourteen-year-old Lexus quit. My wife and I had been married for less than one year and we were struggling to keep up with rent and rising gas prices, so we were not prepared to add a car note to our budget. When the car stalled, I was angry and wanted to vent my frustrations. Instead, I prayed.

I sang, read psalms, and prayed over and over again. I told God I needed more time. I reminded Him that He has all knowledge and power—enough to breathe life into a dying car. If He could speak the world into existence and give men the knowledge to design the vehicle in the first place, then He could certainly fix it.

As I prayed, I felt a strange sense of contentment. When I was through, I thanked God for hearing and granting my prayer and went about my business, no longer stressing about the car.

The next day I started the vehicle and drove to work—forgetting there was a transmission problem to begin with. I did the same thing the day after, the next week, and the next month. I drove the car for a total of two months before the transmission went out again. And when it did, it happened *exactly* as it did the first time, with the same symptoms, as if to remove any doubt from my mind about having a bad transmission two months prior.

Was it just coincidence? Did the transmission just misbehave the first time—give me an early warning—only to really fail two months later? Possibly. I cannot deny this as an option. But that is *not* what I believe happened. I believe that, weak as I am in my wobbly, shaky faith, God moved upon my prayer, and added two months to the life of my dying car.

When we pray in faith God makes special arrangements for us. Not always right away, not always as we expect, but He always changes *something*, because prayer works. He has reprogrammed nature, made the sun stop in the skies, created a dirt path in the middle of the sea, caused iron to float, made fire to fall from the skies, led a man to walk on water, and raised the dead, all because people like you and me—who waste away "'like something rotten, like a garment eaten by moths'" (Job 13:28); who are "'vile and corrupt, who drinks up evil like water!'" (Job 15:16)—were bold enough to ask and believe He would answer!

Faith channels the power of the almighty God and brings it to our dimension; lack of faith limits His power to the little box of our conceptions. God will only go as far as your faith can reach. If you limit Him to your narrow conception, then that's as far as He will go for you. But if yours is faith in action—if your faith is fit, can bench-press twice your weight, and continues to hit the gym until it transcends the weight of the world—then there is no limit to how magnificently God's power will be manifested on your behalf. He will rewrite the laws of nature, if only for an instant, and perform awe-inspiring wonders just because you—yeah, *you*, with your inconsistencies, failings and frailties—had the audacity to trust Him.

2

REACHING WITH A PURPOSE

I F NEWSPAPERS WERE around in her day, her story would have made the front page.

The *Daily News* and *Times* of the ancient world would have featured stories with detailed coverage of the woman whose name had become tantamount to a curse.

For more than a decade she had been shut out from society due to a rare disease. Over the years the illness had drained her strength, her peace of mind, and her financial resources. Using today's terms we would say she sold her stocks, mortgaged her home, liquidated her 401(k), and borrowed money from friends, family, and neighbors to pay the medical professionals, hoping to find a cure, to no avail.

At some point the insurance company refused to pay for additional treatments and began to deny her claims. Her employer gave her the pink slip after a three-month medical leave. The research institutes and drug manufacturers got tired of her constant pleadings; the hottest new drugs provided no relief. Instead they left her with an assortment of side effects. Meanwhile the debt collectors circled around like vultures, threatening her to pay up or suffer their wrath!

For a while a few friends and family remained loyal, but as her condition grew worse, they became weary of taking care of her and loaning her money, and began to distance themselves. Folks from church, who used to pray for and visit with her grew impatient, contesting that *she* must have done something to contract the malady. Because the disease was contagious, her children were compelled to stay away; they could not even hug their mother.

It reached the point where the woman simply wanted to throw in the towel. Medication did not work, prayer did not seem to work, nor did fasting. God seemed to have skipped town, to have forgotten to show mercy. It seemed there was nothing left to do but crawl into a hole and wait to die . . . until, *viva voce*, she heard about a "specialist" she had not yet tried.

He was not your typical doctor. It turned out the man had no medical degree and had never even attended college. But folks said his hands worked wonders. You didn't need to give him lengthy discourses about your condition or wait for hours in his office for a diagnosis. You didn't need to pee into a cup, get an MRI, or draw blood for lab work. This specialist was known to speak to infirmities and touch them away, spit on them and make them disappear. Yes, she was flat broke, but his was a price she could afford—*faith!* Hearing about him gave her an unusual idea. "I'll just touch His clothes and *I will be healed!*" she concluded (Matthew 9:19, paraphrased).

Weak from blood loss after a twelve-year bout of hemorrhaging, her breathing a labored chore, the woman did whatever was necessary to track Jesus down, and eventually she found Him sandwiched in a vast throng. She attempted to make her way to Him, but folks in the crowd scolded her for trying to "cut in." They shoved her aside, thrust her out of their way, so that she stumbled and sprawled awkwardly to the ground.

It was risky for her to be out there. Should someone recognize her, it would be grounds for humiliation and public reprimand. There were laws about these things; people in her condition were required to remain in isolation (see Leviticus 15:25-27), so she had no right to be in public.

But the woman did not care.

She picked herself up and stumbled on until she finally came close enough to touch Christ. This was it—healing was in sight! As she reached for Him, the Master slipped away. Disappointed she slumped to the ground, gasping for air, as people in the crowd bumped into her and stepped on her fingers. She was weak; perspiration mingled with tears rolled down her cheeks, and the crowd became a blur. "Why not give up?" a little voice in her head whispered. "You are out of strength, out of place, out of options."

But the woman decided she would not let Christ get away. Today was *her* day, *her* opportunity to meet the Savior; she would *not* go home unhealed. As the Master headed past her, she sprang forward with all the strength she could muster and managed to brush against the edge of His robe with a fingertip, just seconds before He took another big step.

That's all she needed.

In the blink of an eye incredible power penetrated her, as though all the energies of the sun had filtered through her finger and jolted her body with a burst of vigor. But it wasn't the sun's energy—it was the *Son's!*

She looked at her once dry, pale skin, which now had a fresh, healthy color. She felt transformed, no longer gasping, able to breathe easily again. She tried standing straight, bending left and right, front and back, turning round and round—no aching. She could move easily again—a feeling she had forgotten. The woman was exhilarated, awestricken. Then she grew fearful and began crying....

Meanwhile the crowd moved on.

FAITH IS THE CONDUIT FOR GOD'S GRACE

BRIDGES fascinate me. I believe them to be engineering marvels.

In its simplest form, a bridge provides safe passage over an obstacle, whether a valley, a set of railroad tracks, a river, or another bridge. The type of obstacle and particularly its size, typically determines which of the three major bridge types is used: beam, arch, or suspension.

Bridges vary from the simple to the simply amazing. Some are designed for pedestrian or biker crossings while others are made to bear the weight of cars, trains, and even boats. They vary in shapes and sizes and can do more than simply span physical obstacles. They connect streets, cities, states, countries, even continents. Bringing together architects, artists, and engineers, many bridges have become cultural phenomena. If there were a Hall of Fame for bridges, these next structures would be inductees.

The Golden Gate Bridge, which connects the northern tip of the San Francisco peninsula to Marin County in California, is considered an engineering marvel. The signature orange color, the tremendous towers and main cables make it a delight to behold. It is considered by many to be top among the most amazing bridges in the world.

The Akashi-Kaikyō Bridge is another record holder that deserves our attention. Bridge lengths are measured by the distance they can cross in a single span.* Based on current technology, a suspension bridge is capable of spanning between 2,000 and 7,000 feet.[7] The Akashi-Kaikyō Bridge (Pearl Bridge), linking the city of Kobe to Awaji Island in Japan, has pushed the envelope. It currently has the longest single span in the world—a record 6,532 feet.

The Millau Viaduct, which spans the Valley of the Tarn River in Millau, France, holds the record as the tallest road bridge in the world. Its deck soars 890 feet into the air, and it is said that drivers feel as though they are sailing through the clouds when crossing

* A span is the distance between two bridge supports.

22

this bridge. One of its seven concrete piers is the tallest structure in France—taller than even the Eiffel Tower.

And what bridge lover would not be dazzled by the beauties of the Seri Wawasan Bridge in Putrajaya, Malaysia; the Tower Bridge in London, England; the Sydney Harbour Bridge in Sydney, Australia; or the beautiful Pont Neuf (New Bridge), built in the heart of France in 1607? But these breathtaking structures fade in comparison to this next Bridge.

Spanning the Abyss

If there is one thing the Old Testament makes clear it is that, although God always lingered near His people—a pillar of cloud during the day and a pillar of fire at night for Israel in the Desert of Sinai—there remained an incredible distance between Him and mortal man.

God is "the blessed and only Ruler" the Bible says, "the King of kings and Lord of lords, who alone is immortal and who lives in unapproachable light, whom no one has seen or can see" (1 Timothy 6:15, 16). Kings have been struck by malignant, incurable scourges for ignoring His express commands (2 Chronicles 26:19); priests have fallen dead, burned to death *in the temple,* for apparent minor missteps in how they conducted His services (Leviticus 10:1, 2). "'You cannot see my face,'" Gold told Moses bluntly, "'for no one may see me and live'" (Exodus 33:20). It was to the point where the Jews would not so much pronounce God's awesome name.

How do you relate to a God like that? *Talk to us yourself, and we'll listen to you,* the Israelites told Moses after God came down to Mount Sinai to speak with them. "'Don't let God speak directly to us, or we will die!'" (Exodus 20:19, NLT).

God was the great fearsome One, the God out there, the One whose voice caused fear and trembling and whose presence caused death. They needed a mediator, a go-between, a way of relating to God without fear of being turned into a heap of ash, without saying, "Woe is me, I am ruined!"

Enter Jesus.

What the Golden Gate Bridge is to the northern San Francisco peninsula and Marin County, Jesus is to God and us. He is the great Connector, the One who makes fellowship with God possible. He is the massive structure that spans the abyss sin created between a perfect, holy God and sinful human beings, the great pillar upon which our faith is founded.

Christ brought God incredibly close. We are no longer on separate islands, cut off from Him; the gulf has been bridged. He is no longer the God whose name cannot be spoken. From now on He is Abba, Father. He is our *Daddy*, our *Papa!* God now has a face. He can be touched, and can physically touch us. He can speak to our infirmities, touch our leprosy, grab the hands of our dead and bring them back to life.

"Jesus offered a long, slow look at the face of God" Philip Yancey writes. "If I wonder how God views deformed or disabled people, I can watch Jesus among the crippled, the blind, and those with leprosy. If I wonder about the poor, and whether God has destined them to lives of misery, I can read Jesus' words in the Sermon on the Mount. And if I ever wonder about the appropriate 'spiritual' response to pain and suffering, I can note how Jesus responded to his own: with fear and trembling, with loud cries and tears."[8]

Christ is the One "through whom we have gained access by faith into this grace in which we now stand" (Romans 5:2). He is the full package of God's grace in bodily form (Colossians 2:9), "the mystery of God...in whom are hidden all the treasures of wisdom and knowledge" (verses 2, 3). In spanning the abyss of sin Jesus makes our faith possible, and in so doing, He offers a conduit to receive God's grace.

Faith is the opening through which God sends us all that heaven desires to bestow upon the children of men. It is the conduit though which a man, lost in the forest of his unrighteousness, garbed in his own iniquities, can find his way back to God. We are saved by grace, true, but that grace comes to us through the aperture of faith (Ephesians 2:8). And faith required that God stoop.

The Potentate of the universe—whose glory enshrouds the sea of glass with thick smoke, the God whom the highest heavens are not sufficient to contain—stooped down, and down, lower than the angels (Hebrews 2:7, 9), until He became a fetus. Here is Yancey again:

> The God who fills the universe imploded to become a peasant baby who, like every infant who has ever lived, had to learn to walk and talk and dress himself. In the Incarnation, God's Son deliberately "handicapped" himself, exchanging omniscience for a brain that learned Aramaic phoneme by phoneme, omnipresence for two legs and an occasional donkey, omnipotence for arms strong enough to saw wood but too weak for self-defense. Instead of overseeing a hundred billion galaxies at once, he looked out on a narrow valley in Nazareth, a pile of rocks in the Judean desert, or a crowded street in Jerusalem.[9]

Faith is possible because God stooped—low enough to become a human being, low enough to suffer and die. He stooped to the lowest, deepest, darkest depth of depravity by enveloping Himself with the sins that every single human being ever committed and will commit for all ages and times, to build a bridge over sin's perilous chasm with His atoning sacrifice. Remove Christ from the picture and what remains is a broken road that leads nowhere. Without Him we are left with a useless, ineffective, shipwrecked faith.

GROWING PAINS

NO one ever feeds steaks to a newborn baby.

When babies are born you don't feed them pasta, chicken, rice, or whole potatoes. Instead you start with breastmilk, then with slushy, gooey foods that their systems can handle. The food gets mashed, pureed, liquefied, and strained before it is fed to these precious bundles of joy. They are fed what is easily digestible and super smooth in texture.

As babies grow and become more experienced eaters, the liquids are reduced and the texture of the food is thickened gradually. Things like minced meats are introduced (if you are a meat eater). Or they are fed mashed eggs and avocados. As they get closer to their first year you start giving them whole milk, yogurts, cheeses, and pasta, for example. And before long these tiny people grow into young adults who can walk into a restaurant and order a T-bone steak.

God treats new Christians like we treat our newborn babies. They usually get quick answers to their prayers. Satan is kept at bay, prohibited from constantly pestering them. They tend to be on fire for the Lord, eager to turn the whole world into Christians. They see faith mostly in its majesty and grandeur: they experience glamorous faith.

Glamorous faith is when everything appears to go well—prayers get answered right away, problems are kept in check, favors are granted upon request. But as new Christians begin to mature they learn more about God's character, His mysterious ways, and unconventional methods of dealing with His children. Then little by little things begin to change, until they are dealt the "raw-deal faith."

God begins to treat them like mature adults. He ceases to cuddle, feed, clothe, and hold them by the hand. Eventually they have to grow up and learn to stand on their own. But maturity not only takes time, it also hurts. As they grow up in faith they experience moments of extreme testing. God appears to be aloof, even uncaring, at times. Answers to prayers seem rarer; they sometimes feel alone, confused, discouraged.

Os Guinness writes in his book *The Call*, "In the beginning of our discipleship we think we know all about Jesus. Abandoning everything for him is a dawn-fresh delight, but now as the day wears on, we are not so sure. He is out front and the look on his face is strange."[10]

Many cannot handle a God who does not give them what they want, when they want it. Besides, the preacher promised "God answers *every* prayer!" Their Christian friends insist He performs great miracles and gives financial blessings upon request. "All you have to do is ask!" they say. So these folks come to the faith expecting it to remain glamorous, and feel duped when their expectations are not met. The reality is that glamorous faith is part of the Christianity Welcome Kit. It is sort of an orientation to life with Christ.

During Jesus' earthly ministry the disciples experienced glamorous faith. They saw almost daily tokens of His power. Every day He was healing sickness, commanding nature, forgiving sins, casting out demons, or raising dead people. But when He left for heaven, things changed. Their relationship with Him firmly established, certain that He was truly the Son of God, they quickly received the full measure of the raw-deal faith. Then the persecution started...imprisonment, floggings, martyrdom.

On the surface it is difficult to distinguish glamorous faith from its counterpart raw-deal faith. That's because many people with glamorous faith appear to be as daring and reckless as raw-deal faith. They jump into harm's way, laugh in the face of danger, trust God to do the impossible, and as a result experience spectacular signs and wonders (such as Peter walking on water). Philip Yancey calls this childlike faith, "when a person swallows the impossible.... This is the 'seed faith' that can feed a houseful of orphans or move a mountain, and the Bible contains many proddings toward such."[11]

The problem with glamorous faith is that it has no depth. It focuses not on God's Person, nature or divinity, but mostly on His greatness, power, and ability. This kind of faith is not about relationship; it's not about following God because He is God, because He has made and redeemed us. It is mostly about the "stuff" that God can give; this is the kind of faith that Satan accused Job of possessing.

Unfortunately for us today, many ministers promote only the glamour of faith. They promise a God who ushers us to "the top of the world" where He caters to our every whim. They insist that He meets all of our needs upon request, performs supernatural wonders whenever we need Him to, heals every sickness, answers every prayer. "If you don't experience such things it's because you don't have faith," they conclude. Many churchgoers today would suffer great disappointments and would call you a pagan if you told them that faith is not about on-demand miracles, vending-machine blessings and problem-free existence.

God does not spend much time on glamorous faith. It is the little preview package that He hands out to fresh, green, still-wet-behind-the-ears Christians. But once you've gotten settled He gets right down to business, introducing you to the raw-deal faith. "The kind of faith God values seems to develop best when everything fuzzes over, when God stays silent, when the fog rolls in."[12]

It is a sign of immaturity for any Christian to insist on miracles and blessings all the time. It means he is still in the infancy stage of his faith, follows God for the glamour—faith with benefits.

Don't get me wrong. Raw-deal faith is not all work and no play. God does not push you into a dungeon, throw away the keys, and call that faith. To the contrary, when your faith has matured to raw-deal status, the benefits are so abundant that you sometimes take them for granted; the miracles are so prevalent they become the norm (think of the disciples healing paralytics, raising the dead). The difference is, you no longer need them to believe. They *ensue* from your belief rather than precede them; they are the result of trusting God and not a condition for it.

Miracles Do Not Lead to Faith

"Well, wait a minute! Are you saying that my faith is weak if I expect miracles? Does that mean that if my car's brakes failed and I was heading toward a cliff I should not pray for God to stop the car and save my life?" If the plane's engines sputter to a halt at 37,000 feet, you want God to show up immediately, guide that plane safely to a runway, and save everyone aboard. You expect a cure for your cancer, and you want that loved one to miraculously recover from Parkinson's. Is it a lack of faith to expect God to perform incredible wonders for us?

The fact is, the Lord performs hundreds, maybe thousands, of miracles just to keep us alive every single day. The devil makes it his mission to ensure that every single circumstance works toward our demise. God's angels must work diligently around the clock to prevent or undo his handiwork. We just don't see the war waged between those two agencies because they are fought behind the scenes in the realm of the spirit.

My point is this: it's not wrong to expect miracles from God because He is already performing them on your behalf every day. His grace is what keeps you alive. Expecting your loving Father to love you is not wrong at all. Jesus Himself makes it clear that we should expect God's blessings (Matthew 7:9–11).

The problem arises when these blessings become entitlements, when miracles become a condition for faith. Expecting God to show Himself off to you, to prove His Godhood as it were, before you accept Him, will set you up for failure because miracles do little to grow our faith. Just ask the nation of Israel.

If any nation has had physical, final proof of God's constant presence and ability to give "stuff," it was Israel. From the moment Moses stepped onto the scene and announced God had sent him to set them free, and throughout their desert wanderings, the Israelites experienced repeated, daily expressions of God's power.

Israel left Egypt on the heels of ten devastating plagues (Exodus 7–12). They watched as the impassable waters of the Red Sea split in half and two great liquid walls and a dry dirt highway emerged. With their own dusty leather sandals they walked between the walls of seawater and made it to the other side of the desert (Exodus 14:21, 22).

God's presence shielded them from the furnace-like desert heat in the form of a pillar of clouds by day and protected them from the blistering cold in the form of a pillar of fire by night (Exodus 13:21, 22; 14:19, 20).

Every day they digested the manna, food of angels (Psalm 78:25), which fell for them day in, day out, for forty long years in the desert (Exodus 16:13-15, 35).

The clothes they had when they left Egypt endured for forty years without wearing out (Deuteronomy 8:4; 29:5). God made water gush from rocks—twice—to quench their parched throats (Exodus 17:5-8; Numbers 20:8-11).

Yet how did Israel respond to all of these incredible wonders?

There they were, standing before the Red Sea, with the memory of the incredible miracles of the ten plagues fresh on their minds, grumbling because of Pharaoh's pursuit. "'Was it because there were no graves in Egypt that you brought us to the desert to die? What have you done to us by bringing us out of Egypt? Didn't we say to you in Egypt, "Leave us alone; let us serve the Egyptians"?'" (Exodus 14:11, 12).

After they crossed the Red Sea they grumbled for lack of potable water: "'What shall we drink?'" (Exodus 15:24, NASB). Then for food: "'If only we had died by the Lord's hand in Egypt! There we sat around pots of meat and ate all the food we wanted, but you have brought us out into this desert to starve this entire assembly to death'" (16:3). On and on the list goes, from complaints about life in the wilderness (Numbers 11:1), to complaints about the lack of meat in their diet (verses 4–6), to complaints about the giants in Canaan (Numbers 14:2, 3).

Philip Yancey laments, "God did not play hide-and-seek with the Israelites; they had every proof of his existence you could ask for. But astonishingly—and I could hardly believe this result, even as I read it—God's directness seemed to produce the very *opposite* of the desired effect. The Israelites responded not with worship and love, but with fear and open rebellion. God's visible presence did nothing to improve lasting faith."[13]

This is a wake-up call to all who expect God to perform miraculous wonders on-demand to satisfy their curiosity. Miracles, however impressive and ostentatious, do nothing to increase our love for God. As Fyodor Dostoevsky says, the heart bent on disbelief "will always find strength and ability to disbelieve in the miraculous, and if he is confronted with a miracle as an irrefutable fact he would rather disbelieve his own senses than admit the fact."

Although miracles do not suddenly make us love God more, they do serve other purposes. They reinforce our belief in God, build on faith that we already have. God may also use miracles to correct misconceptions about Himself, as in the case of Saul of Tarsus. But He will not waste time proving Himself to people who blatantly refuse to obey Him or demand miracles before they "grace" Him with their faith (see Mathew 12:38, 39).

"Would a burst of miracles nourish faith? Not the kind of faith

God seems interested in, evidently. The Israelites give ample proof that signs may only addict us to signs, not to God."[14]

If you are waiting for God to use miracles to convince you to have faith, I am sorry to report you will be sorely disappointed. God is not interested in impressing you with His powers. As the Gospels show, He performed miracles to help love take root, much like irrigating soil will help plants grow. Performing miracles for a barren heart with no love or devotion toward God would be like irrigating an empty, idle plot of land and expecting it to suddenly produce good crops without ever sowing a single seed. That's not going happen.

REACHING WITH A PURPOSE

REACH \'rēch\, transitive verb, "to stretch out: extend" (Merriam-Webster).

To reach is to expand yourself, to broaden your horizon, to lengthen your extremities. Reaching involves stretching beyond yourself, relocating your boundaries. You cannot reach without some degree of pain or discomfort, because reaching strains you. It has a wrenching about it, a straining about it. It demands the use of some force, involves pressure and trauma. To reach is to expose yourself, to make yourself vulnerable to failure, vulnerable to a fall. In order to reach, you must be willing to be displaced.

The story of the woman at the beginning of this chapter is recorded in Matthew 9 and Mark 5. We met her at a critical time, while Jesus was responding to a 9-1-1 call from Jairus, a prominent temple official, on behalf of his dying daughter (Mark 5:22, 23). He was sandwiched between hundreds of people who were eager to hear Him speak. The crippled, blind, and mute, the poor, the sinners, and those plagued with all manner of infirmities—they were all vying for His attention, touching Him, and begging Him for favor. No doubt the throng also included society's elite—rich businessmen such as Joseph of Arimathea; Pharisees such as Nicodemus; and perhaps other more influential men of faith. But of all the people rudely shoving the Lord from side to side, no one reached out to Him for power and healing the way this woman did.

She came physically weak, discouraged, and scourged with an embarrassing ailment. She was deemed an outcast, a prisoner in her own skin. The woman had not been around Jesus as long as these folks had, perhaps she had never even physically seen Him before. But she came with a purpose, and because of it, she received greater blessings than even the disciples!

The woman was certainly not the only person reaching for Jesus that day; there were others reaching for Him as well. Some reached for Him to hear His words of life. Many intellectuals had come to reach for Him too, but their motive was to challenge Him, to question His divinity, to embarrass and entrap Him. Some were reaching for Him simply to see if the talk buzzing about Him in the media was true. Others came because He had become a local celebrity, and they wanted to size Him up. Still others came just looking for something to gossip about. But this woman came for the purpose of obtaining grace.

With her mind made up, the woman came because she *knew* that when she reached for Christ she would grab something. And what a reach it was! The moment she touched Him Christ stopped dead in His tracks, as though He had hit a brick wall, and asked what must have seemed like a ridiculous question to those around Him. Bounced around like a Ping-Pong ball in the thick crowd, Christ demanded: "Who touched Me?"

People stared at Jesus as if He had three heads. "Have You seen this crowd?" Peter asked. "How can You ask, 'Who touched Me?' We *all* touched You!" But Christ knew something that Peter and the others did not. He physically felt "that power had gone out from him" (Mark 5:30). So Christ scanned the crowd, His eyes settled on the woman, and He stared intently at her.

When the woman reached for Jesus she did in fact grab something: she took hold of infinite power! Like a giant magnet, her faith drew signals of omnipotence from Christ, channeled it through her fingers, and spread it all over her body. The blast of energy was so powerful that it immediately neutralized her infirmities, bringing about instantaneous and complete healing (verse 29).

There was nothing magical about Christ's clothes. I imagine His clothing was no different from Simon Peter's or Judas Iscariot's. She could have decided on Christ's sandals, His shadow, His sweat, or the dust that He trod. It was not an issue of how she reached or of what she touched. Rather, it was an issue of the purpose of her reach, the resolute determination that God had already granted her healing, and it would be hers if only she asked, or in this case, *reached* for it! It was an issue of her faith.

Faith requires that we reach, but when we do, our reach must have purpose.

Purpose infuses life into our faith. "Daniel *purposed* in his heart that he would not defile himself" (Daniel 1:8, KJV), and that was that. Allurements, bribes, threats, intimidation, and even the lion's den—nothing would deter him from his purpose. Purpose is what gives our faith a backbone. It is what enables us to stand, what keeps us going when the tides of life thrust us way off course. It is purpose that keeps the tired, weary legs going when the steps are heavy and the mountain's summit is nowhere in sight.

Purpose renders our faith consistent, enabling us to persist in spite of how high the odds are stacked against us. It creates a surge in our hearts, develops a stubborn, relentless resolve that empowers us to plow forward and blast through obstacles. Even when rebuked, misunderstood, or when those who should support us urge us to give up the fight, purpose keeps us going, such that we will jump higher, run faster, or cry louder, as in the case of blind Bartimaeus (see Mark 10:47, 48).

Before we reach, a decision is made as to what the result of our faith will be. From that point on, no matter how dismal our circumstances or how vain our attempts, we reach until our faith fructifies. We reach when it seems as though the abyss that separates us from our desire is infinite. We reach when hope has waned and we are urged to ask, *what's the use?* With boldness we still reach, even when we are at the end of our reach, even when the arm we've extended can reach no further.

Nevertheless we reach, because somehow faith convinces us that God can shatter the walls of impossibility if we have the audacity to reach with purpose! It makes us do what looks foolish, propels us to places others would never venture. In our mind's eye we see the healing, deliverance, mercy, and grace, and we extend ourselves to grab it.

Gauging the Limits of your Reach

Despite the fact that some bridges are massive concrete structures that weigh tons, they are able to stretch and condense in order to withstand two major forces that act upon them: compression (which causes them to contract) and tension (which causes them to stretch or expand). Bridge designers must take these forces into consideration during the design phase in order to prevent these structures from buckling or snapping.

You cannot exercise faith in your comfort zone. There *has* to be a stretch. Faith takes you into the unknown. It cannot be faith if it is comfortable, if you already know from physical evidence what is going to happen next, and it cannot be faith if you do not reach beyond where you have reached before. That is why faith is an exercise. God will test your limits every single time you stretch the sinews of your faith.

The woman with the hemorrhaging issue went through a lot of trouble to find Christ that day. After hearing about Him, she went on a quest for Jesus that may have lasted several days. Commentators suggest that she began searching for Jesus in Capernaum at the lakeshore where He had been teaching (see Mark 5:21) and missed Him. She later learned that He was at Matthew's home and went there, but alas, she arrived too late again. When she finally caught up to Him, the crowd around Him created an obstacle, making it almost impossible to reach Him. Her embarrassing disease, her weakened physical condition, the law; all presented major hindrances that she needed to overcome. God stretched her limits to the point where, as one author puts it, she began to despair and was ready to throw in the towel. Even in the presence of the Great Healer, her limits were still being tested.

God knows your limits better than any architect or engineer. He knows how far you can reach, and can also control the forces acting against you to prevent buckling and snapping. But He will stretch your limits—of that you may be certain. You should also take comfort, because He will never allow you to buckle or snap.

Do not despair when there seems to be no hope—when it seems as though you have reached the end of human strength, when it seems your arms can stretch no further. When you look on the horizon and see nothing but dark clouds hovering above your world, remember your Great Architect, and purpose in your heart to reach for the impossible!

LAST WORDS
When God Delays...

FROM MY JOURNAL: SEPTEMBER 2006

I began my first job while I was still in college. When I graduated and began pursuing my master's degree, my employer promised that upon graduation they would promote me and give me a pay increase. However, when I graduated the story changed. Instead, they offered me another position that they had been unable to fill for some time. It would have been a lateral move with no pay increase, and accepting that job would have led to career stagnation.

When I realized this I decided to find another job. I began praying, fasting, and looking for other opportunities within and outside of the organization, but could not find anything. Weeks turned to months and months to years. To make matters worse, things kept changing at work. I got tossed from one boss to another—four in as many years. Frustrations and tensions mounted. Some managers treated me like a child, yanking things from my hands and throwing them into the trash; others yelled and bullied me. I felt as if I could not stay at that job one more hour, but God kept me there for three more years. When it finally came time to get me out of there, the Lord gave me two job offers at once. Prayerfully my wife and I made a selection, and as they say, the rest is history.

Why did God wait so long to give me a new job? Why the delay?

This seems to be a constant for the typical praying person. True, there are times when answers to our prayers come like a speeding bullet. However, for the most part, God appears to sit on His hands—to take His time while things get worse, and wait until situations get out of control before He decides to jump in and do something. He waited 400 years before finally delivering Israel from Egyptian bondage; He waited twelve years before healing the woman of her hemorrhage; and He took His sweet time on the short walk to Jairus' home, to the point that his daughter died by the time Christ arrived. Even with Lazarus, His *friend*, Jesus waited four days, until the man died and was buried. Now He is probably taking His time with your cancer, unemployment, or rocky marriage. But does God delay? Can we really say He takes too long?

As created beings, our concept of time is so different from God's that we sometimes get frustrated with His pace and accuse Him of slacking. To us time is a commodity of finite, limited duration that breaks life down into small increments. It inches forward in a sequential pattern, one increment following the next in perfect succession. It hedges us between walls of past and future, providing a window into the past while blinding us to the events of tomorrow. We get to experience time just once, before it disappears into the archives of history. We could never imagine a world without wristwatches, calendars, or appointments. We are concerned about the minutes (except for the slackers), and rightly so, because they turn into hours, days, months, and years, and our bodies respond with wrinkles, arthritis, degeneration, and death.

God, on the other hand, is not limited by the walls of time. He has been around since before there was time (Psalm 90:2), and set it in motion when He pronounced the memorable words, "'Let there be light!'" (Genesis 1:3). God has no beginning and no end. We are each given a set amount of time, each have an expiration date. Not God—His "years will never end" (Psalm 102:27). Everything lays bare before His eyes. One glance at you and He captures it all: birth, life, and death. The future stretches before Him with perfect clarity; nothing is hidden from His sight.

Because God sees into eternity, He knows how events coincide and what consequences they produce. He sees, with unencumbered clarity, the precise moment when an event needs to take place to produce the most excellent result. God always takes the human element into consideration. When He sets the date and time for deliverance, our responses and the results thereof change the outcome. In order to secure the best outcome He sometimes moves the target or changes the deadline. At least that's the way it would appear from our vantage point.

But impatient as we are, we often sacrifice results for temporary relief. We want an answer now, *today*, even if we are not ready for it. What we call a "delay" may be God's way of perfecting circumstances. He knows if you are going to be hardheaded, rebellious, lazy, or irresponsible, and He takes that into consideration when setting the date and time of your deliverance.

I discovered, after leaving my first employer to join the second, that there was a reason why God kept me back those three years. During that dreaded period of waiting, I gained a critical set of skills that made me a valuable player in my next role. During the first three years with my new employer we managed to double productivity, cut inventory in half, increase profit, reduce footprint by thirty-five percent, and navigate through the worst economic downturn of our generation without a hitch. After being forced to get through the recession with only half of our production staff, the company did not hire a single person (except to replace a couple of retirees) when business came roaring back, even when orders exceeded pre-recession levels.

It's hard to understand what good can possibly come from your suffering. Job had the same problem when he lost ten children and his entire fortune in one day. Looking at suffering through our lenses we can never understand its true purpose; we can never comprehend how it fits into God's plan. So let's surrender ourselves to Him and trust Him to help us navigate through the storm. When Christ appears to lollygag for a couple extra days, months, or years, it's not because He does not care and it's not because He wants you to squirm. It is "'so that you may believe,'" (John 11:15); so that your faith may increase.

God does not delay!

MATURITY

3

DIVINE INCONVENIENCE

YOU WILL NOT find his name in Scripture's Hall of Faith. He was not as famous as Moses, the great deliverer of the Hebrews from Egyptian bondage, nor as admired as David, the man after God's own heart (1 Samuel 13:14). He was not credited with preserving the human race during earth's greatest deluge, nor did he preach the 120-year evangelical campaign that Noah is famous for.

Nevertheless he stands shoulder-to-shoulder with Scripture's greatest men of faith.

The Bible calls him "a just man," or *dikaios* (Greek). He was a man who observed the rules and customs of Scriptures, a righteous man. He was an adamant observer of the laws and rabbinical traditions. Although not very popular, he was well known in his tight-knit community as a man of impeccable repute, a God-fearing man who sets the standard for other men. He was not a preacher, but knew the Word very well, followed the law to the letter, and mentored others with his teachings. Life did not afford him many luxuries, but it was a good life, one he invested so much of himself to build, and which had a future meticulously planned…until God came and messed it up!

FAITH NEEDS CONSTRUCTION

IF you have ever traveled on a road under construction, you know how inconvenient that can be.

The pavement is uneven, making your car unstable and more difficult to control. The road is narrower and construction vehicles and crews litter the place. The smell of tarmac fills the air, the bright lighting used after sunset can be blinding, and the clanging and rattling of the tools and equipment is enough to give you a headache. Traffic becomes a nightmare as hundreds of cars attempt to squeeze through one lane on highways where six would normally be inadequate.

But the wear and tear caused by the weight of heavy vehicles, and the effects of sun, rain, and snow, leave road surfaces full of cracks and potholes. This deterioration makes roads impassable and dangerous over time, and construction becomes necessary to maintain and repair them.

Faith is no different. Whether we are talking about a brand new Christian or a forty-year veteran preacher, our faith requires repairs and maintenance.

Life is filled with burdens that weigh heavily on our shoulders. The rush of circumstances beat constantly against us. Relationships, conditions at work, issues of health and money, all of these can, even in subtle ways, cause faith to deteriorate. God knows where the cracks and potholes reside in our faith, and He places it under construction to repair the damages.

The construction process is neither convenient nor easy. It introduces detours, sharp turns, dead ends, unevenness, ditches, and brokenness to what we often wish was a smooth, normal life. God interrupts our lives and ruins our comfort in order to build us into people after His own heart. Yes, He takes us as He finds us. But then as a sculptor carves a stone block into a masterpiece, God chisels away our rough edges until we become capable of serving His purpose, until He creates in us the character of Jesus Christ.

Necessary Emptiness

Doug Bachelor writes, "The light of Jesus cannot burn in a heart that is full with other things. The oil of God's spirit can be poured only into empty vessels."[15]

Contents have the tendency to hide the cracks and imperfections in our characters. When we are full we tend to miss the goo and slime that permeate our lives. Faith construction requires emptiness. While our gifts and talents remain—our eloquence, intellect, and education—our attitudes cannot reflect those who parade their endowments ostentatiously. Emptiness changes us. It leaves us exposed, magnifies our defects, pointedly revealing the brutal reality that something is wrong with us. God removes the contents and exposes our shame. He brings us to realize that we are nothing before making something out of us, empties us completely before filling us back up.

Moses was not always the calm, loving, patient man who was "more humble than anyone else on the face of the earth" (Numbers 12:3). He was once a hothead who would literally have given you a dirt nap if you pushed him over the edge (see Exodus 2:11, 12). Even after his faith's construction, traces of his anger remained, such that he would sometimes get "hot with anger" (Exodus 11:8; see also 32:19, 20). Before making him governor of His people, God first put Moses' faith under construction.

Young, handsome, rich and famous, Moses was a prince, the adopted son of Pharaoh's powerful daughter; he was a man who lived in the limelight. Judging by today's celebrity lifestyle, we could expect Moses' every move to be watched, his face to grace every magazine and tabloid stand. A prospective successor to the throne, this powerful eligible bachelor had hundreds of servants catering to his every whim.

Moses had a sharp mind and knowledge of Egyptian literature and science. He had been an army commander who led military campaigns in foreign lands. He knew the strengths and weaknesses of the Egyptian armed forces, and was uniquely qualified and capable, at least on the surface, to lead Israel out of Egyptian bondage.

But Moses' self-sufficiency was one of his many flaws. He was a battle-tested soldier, trained in military tactics and warfare. When he felt the call to deliver Israel, Moses the soldier showed up before God with his fine résumé and list of credentials, ready to tell the Lord how deliverance ought to be secured. He killed a man and buried his corpse in the sand. Moses thought he would do things *his* way, with the strength of arms. Well, he had something else coming.

God yanked the prince out of the palatial halls of Egypt and thrust him into the desert mountains of Midian, stripping away the lifestyle of privilege. The man who once had bodyguards on every side for protection, who was once chauffeured around the city in a royal motorcade, now walked the dusty desert lands of Midian alone.

The Lord broke Moses down on microscopic levels, peeling off some of his Egyptian customs and influences. His experiences in Egypt had implanted in him habits and character traits that made it impossible for God to use him. He needed new sceneries, new exposures, new circumstances, and one-on-one time with God before he could be made into the man the Lord desired for him to be.[16]

You can imagine the psychological effects of falling from A-list celebrity status to chasing sheep. Instead of Egypt's fine structures, mountains and deserts now surrounded him. No more fine dining, no busy lifestyle. God slowed him down, stripped him naked, and buried him in the backyard of the world—empty, isolated, forgotten. There stood Moses, in the depth of obscurity, with his imperfections exposed and with a large sign over his faith that read *Under Construction!*

Agent of Purification

Heat treatment is a process that is used to modify material properties. It is most commonly used on metals, which are comprised of microscopic crystals known as "grains." Heat treatment is effective because heating an alloy at extreme temperatures affects the size and alignment of the grains, thereby making the metal softer or harder.

Not every material goes through the same type of heat treatment. The type of treatment used—annealing, case hardening, quenching, etc.—depends on the material's original properties and its intended application. The temperature and the atmosphere are controlled to create an environment that produces the right level of hardness or softness. Too little or too much heat, cooling too fast or too slowly, or cooling in air versus in water, can destroy the material or ruin the application.

Notice that fire—an agent of purification—is used to heat treat the metal.

A chemical reaction that results when fuel, oxygen, and an ignition source come together, fire will either consume or improve any material that's exposed to it. It tends to remove impurities, rearrange properties, burn off unwanted defects, or completely incinerate. Things exposed to fire will either become char and ash or they will emerge brighter, stronger, and with superior properties, ready for applications they could never have been fit for without the exposure to the flame.

Like the heat-treater God uses fire—pain, an agent of spiritual purification—to burn the dross from our faith. He employs the pangs of affliction, the acuate end of the chisel of calamity, to chip away at the defects in our characters.

Conflicts come our way not because the Lord is picking on us, nor because of anything we have done wrong.* God often makes us uncomfortable in order to move us from where we are to where He wants to take us, transform us from who we are to the people He desires us to be.

The apostle Peter writes, "In this you greatly rejoice, though now for a little while you may have had to suffer grief in all kinds of trials. These have come so that your faith—of greater worth than gold, which perishes even though refined by fire—may be proved genuine and may result in praise, glory and honor when Jesus Christ is revealed" (1 Peter 1:6, 7).

Dr. Charles Swindoll concurs: "God never puts us through the blast furnace in the desert to ruin us. He does it to refine us. And in the midst of that howling wilderness, through the process of time, the stinging sand bites through the rust and corrosion, and we become a usable tool in His hand."[17]

Pain has a way of shaping its subject, especially when it is deemed unmerited. It will either make you bitter and resentful or create in you a sense of humility and acceptance that increases faith in God. The fire of affliction comes against a man and reveals his true nature, making clear the stuff of which he is made.

Remember, when exposed to the fires of affliction, that God knows your genetic makeup and material composition. He knows how much heat to apply and how long it will take to bring about your superior properties. God will never keep you in the furnace too long, nor will He draw you out too quickly. Ultimately your response in the fire will determine what comes out: char, ash, or a pure, refined, sparkling block of gold.

---

* That is not to say that people do not reap the fruits of their evil acts. Put your hand in fire and you will get burned. However we sometimes experience hardships simply because God is trying to form our character.

Reality Training

Imagine lying on a hospital bed waiting to have brain surgery and having a doctor walk in with a yellow and black textbook in hand entitled, "Idiot's Guide to Brain Surgery"! You straighten up in your bed and demand an explanation, to which the doctor replies, "Don't worry, it's alright. I've been reading books on brain surgery for twenty-five years; I know what I'm doing!" No one in their right mind would trust a textbook expert with brain surgery. God is not content with textbook Christians either. He builds your faith from reality, taking you through a series of training programs designed specifically to shape you up.

If God wants you to write a book about pain, He will not be content to give you Webster's definition of the word. It will not be enough to pull the old encyclopedia volume from your library shelf, dust it off, and look under the letter "P" to dissect the word "Pain."

Rather, the Lord will put you through painful situations, or at least expose you to pain by putting people in your life who are in dire misery, so you can get firsthand experience of what pain truly is. He will teach you to understand pain, to feel its very texture, reel in the pit of hurt and suffering, and show you how to rise from its ashes so that you can teach someone else how to deal with it. God does His schooling from reality; He constructs our faith in the hustle and bustle of daily life.

Moses found himself in the barren desert dealing with sheep—weak, stubborn, uncaring, not-too-bright sheep. Sheep tend to follow the crowd, and will follow each other to their own demise. If a sheep at the front of a line jumps off a cliff, chances are high that the others will follow suit. Sheep don't care about your agenda or feelings or how many times you put your neck on the line for them. They don't pay attention to your needs and will not waste their time focusing on you. If you are patient, kind, and loving enough to deal with sheep, you can put up with just about anyone.

Under the tutelage of Egypt's illustrious teachers, Moses mastered the arts, sciences, literature, and religion. He acquired military training and gained knowledge of civil administration and the law. He "was educated in all the wisdom of the Egyptians and was powerful in speech and action" (Acts 7:22). However, Egypt's educators could not prepare Moses to deal with the stiff-necked Israelites. In the desert he learned patience, self-denial, discipline, obedience, and self-control.

God knew that Moses would deal with the obstinate, selfish, disobedient, and undisciplined Israelites in the barren deserts of Sinai for forty years. He dragged him from the limelight and comfort of Egypt's royal courts and thrust him into the barren deserts of Sinai for forty years, to receive his training from sheep. Talk about reality training! God made him learn for the exact length of time, in the exact environment where he would minister to the Israelites. Don't be surprised if your reality training program is this custom-made as well!

DIVINE INCONVENIENCE

"'LITTLE people like you and me, if our prayers are sometimes granted, beyond all hope and probability, had better not draw hasty conclusions to our own advantage. If we were stronger, we might be less tenderly treated. If we were braver, we might be sent, with far less help, to defend far more desperate posts in the great battle.'"[18]

The statement above was made by C. S. Lewis, as quoted in what is probably my favorite Philip Yancey book: *Disappointment with God*. The average Christian prays for peace and favor, and while there is nothing wrong with either one, we should also realize that God's peace is best experienced in the middle of a storm, and His favor is sometimes draped in grief. As Philip Yancey observes, God reserves His toughest assignments for His closest friends.

As an army general, you would never select a new recruit to lead your troops into battle. You certainly would not pick him for the toughest, most dangerous mission. This you would reserve for an experienced, trustworthy soldier, someone who you are sure would get the job done, someone who would put duty before comfort, who would put nation before self, who would put himself in harm's way to protect the troops and would do whatever is necessary to preserve the union. This is the kind of person you would send after your toughest foe.

Likewise, when God has a difficult assignment He does not select the whiners, the crybabies, or the cowards. God chooses people He can trust, people who, though they may fall, will rise up again, people who will trust Him when there seems to be no reason at all to do so, when it seems as if *He* is the enemy. Those are the kind of men and women that God sends to the front lines, the kind of people to whom He shows His greatest favor.

Joseph was selected for the most amazing assignment any man could ever hope for: he was handpicked to raise God! What great honor it was for him to have the God of the universe call him daddy. Christ was the Word made flesh, "God's thought made audible."[19] He is the Radiance of God's glory, "the exact representation of His nature" (Hebrews 1:3, NASB). "Through him all things were made; without him nothing was made that has been made" (John 1:3). Christ is the superglue that holds the world together (Colossians 1:16, 17; Hebrews 1:3). Without Him the universe would simply disintegrate, for by Him "are all things, and we exist through Him" (1 Corinthians 8:6, NASB).

But in order to redeem sinful humans and to become our

substitute, Christ, the Word, was hewn into human form, metamorphosed from spirit into flesh.

Jesus came to planet earth the way all other babies arrive, and like the rest of us, He needed someone to care for Him. He needed to learn how to respect His elders, how to be a Man. He, like all other children of Adam, would grow to want love, food, shelter, and human companionship. He would endure pain and disappointment, would sweat and ache and bleed. As a Man, Christ was no longer beyond the allurements of the devil, and would need to survive his severest of temptations.

Since children do not learn the things of the world on their own, but need teachers, Jesus needed someone to teach Him how to be a Man. So He picked Joseph for the job. On this righteous man fell the responsibility of inculcating God's virtues into the world's Messiah. It was indeed one of heaven's supreme honors, and was no small task.

The salvation of humanity's greatest men—Abel, Moses, Paul the Apostle, Enoch, Daniel, David, even Abraham—hinged upon Joseph's performance as a father. If he failed, they would fail. Should Joseph somehow impart the wrong character traits into Jesus, such that He succumbed to the smallest possible temptation, the ripple effects would shatter the plan of salvation, and the universe in its entirety would pay the price. Talk about weighty responsibilities! While raising the incarnate God was a special honor and privilege, it would also greatly inconvenience Joseph, requiring from him what was perhaps his most prized possession.

A Tough Choice

Joseph managed to do just fine on a peasant's salary. As a carpenter he made barely enough money to support himself and his family, and took great pains to ensure he did everything right.

Apparently a widower, this righteous man followed the customs of the law to pick a new bride when it was time to remarry.

He found himself a beautiful, respectable virgin and proposed to her. Far from our customs in the Western world today, this marriage proposal required the groom to pay a dowry to the bride's relatives, followed by customary celebrations and a binding contract—a contract that was accompanied with solemn vows.[20] At this point, if the man desired to break off the engagement for any reason, he would need to file for divorce. So Mary was technically Joseph's wife, except they could not live together or consummate their union until the actual marriage celebration.

Joseph picked Mary because he knew her to be a virtuous woman. Imagine his shock and disappointment when she went away for about three months, perhaps leaving him behind to build their future home and furniture, and returned pregnant.

As a righteous man, Joseph lived by the Book. He was not a legalist with a superficial righteousness that compelled him to keep the letter of the law to receive praise from his peers. Joseph's righteousness was deeply rooted in his faith. He lived to please God, not men, and therefore sought to do what was right by Him at all times, regardless of people's responses or of the consequences to himself. This much is evident in his response when he found out how Mary became pregnant. But at this point, as far as Joseph was concerned, some scoundrel in the hill country impregnated his woman, and the *right* thing to do, as a righteous man, was to break off the engagement and not marry an adulteress. He made up his mind to divorce her, but that presented a major problem.

The law was clear on such matters, and being a strict observer of it, Joseph knew only too well that if, after marrying a woman, a man found that his wife had not been a virgin, he had the right to drag her to court and divorce her on those charges. Should his accusations prove true, then "the woman must be taken to the door of her father's home, and there the men of the town must stone her to death" (Deuteronomy 22:13, 14, 20, 21, NLT).

Joseph became cripplingly afraid. He loved Mary dearly, and even when he thought she had broken his trust, he did not want her to die. He was afraid because it seemed that the only way to preserve his reputation was to accuse and divorce Mary, which, in essence, would be like signing her death warrant. She would be stoned to death for committing "a disgraceful crime in Israel by being promiscuous while living in her parents' home" (verse 21, NLT). Joseph was also afraid because doing nothing in order to preserve her life would cost him his good name and reputation as a righteous man, his most prized possession (see Proverbs 22:1).

Many men would have taken this opportunity to drag Mary through a shameful divorce. The local papers and tabloids and comedians would have had a field day with her. Imagine the newspaper headline: "Woman Claims She Slept With God!" Mary would have become the object of shame and ridicule; her death would have been a public spectacle.

Being a *dikaios*, Joseph sought a peaceful resolution. He wanted to break off the engagement without causing Mary any more shame than absolutely necessary, and equally important, while preserving his good name. But how could he preserve both her life and his reputation? As he pondered what to do, Joseph discovered a loophole in the law.

The law made it clear that the woman would be stoned *if* the man "publicly accuses her of shameful conduct" (Deuteronomy 22:14, NLT). However, should he divorce her privately, her life would be spared. So Joseph opted for a private resolution (see Matthew 1:19). But before going through with his plan God showed up and revealed a much bigger plan.

The Faith that Costs Your All

Joseph endured what I call *divine inconvenience*.

This is when faith comes with a hefty price tag. It is when God demands from us our best, the kind of faith that pits us against our worst-case scenarios. Some misconstrue this kind of faith; they deduce from it God's inexistence or carefree attitude, incorrectly painting from their pain the picture of an uncaring God who picks on them on a whim. These conclusions could not be further from the truth.

God is a personal Being who pays major attention to details. He is so intimately involved with His creatures that the very hairs on our heads are numbered (Matthew 10:30). He did not simply throw some strands of hair onto our heads and then go back later to take inventory of them. No! God purposefully decided, before I was born, how many strands of hair, and what color and texture, would work best with the design of Sam Belony's oval-shaped head. And He is this involved with every one of His creatures.

God knows the inventory of water in all of the world's oceans, down to the very last drop. He knows the names of every single ant that roams the face of the earth at any given moment—He knows when they are hungry and He feeds them. He is involved in the lives of the birds and insects, cares when a rat is in pain, and provides for even the grass of the fields. So if calamity somehow finds its way into your mailbox, it's not because God fell asleep on the job.

Before allowing adversity to approach you God measures it, weighs it on a balance, tests it, retests it, validates it, compares it to your strength, takes His stand next to you then, *and only then*, permits it to strike you.

Nevertheless you still feel pain.

To be the father of God, Joseph endured abuse, calumny, and defamation of character. The Incarnation of Christ required his reputation to take a fatal blow, one from which it never recovered. When

Mary began showing and there had been no marriage celebration, or the math did not add up, everyone thought it was Joseph who impregnated her. Even in our day of loose morals, a church elder or deacon who impregnates a woman without marrying her is considered shameful and disappointing. Imagine how that would have been viewed in Joseph's day and culture. That kind of action was a crime against society, one for which people were stoned to death.

From that point forward Joseph could expect to be ostracized. Townsfolk would point at him in the streets and in the marketplaces and whisper. They would censure him, call him a sham, a hoax, and would say that his righteousness had been counterfeit since everyone would think that he fathered an illegitimate child. This was Joseph's nightmare scenario, and it was about to come true. God understood his fears, and sent heaven's highest-ranking angel to reassure him.

"'Do not be afraid'" the angel Gabriel said to Joseph. *This is going to hurt...a lot! But don't be afraid. Your hurt will be a building block in saving the entire human race, vindicating God's character before the unseen world and eternizing His law.* "'Do not be afraid,'" *because your shame will help eternally secure Satan's fate, and ensure the destruction of evil for all eternity. Don't be afraid.* "'Do not be afraid to take Mary home as your wife, because what is conceived in her is from the Holy Spirit. She will give birth to a son, and you are to give him the name Jesus'" (Matthew 1:20, 21).

Gabriel was saying to Joseph: God understands your pain, but your reputation will be collateral damage—a casualty of war—in the great controversy between good and evil. He cares about your hurt, but cannot allow it to defeat His purpose. So don't be afraid; take it like a man of faith. Marry this pregnant woman, and the Baby is yours!

Just as directed, Joseph took it on the chin without complaint. Not once is he recorded blaming or questioning God. He never asked why. Even Mary had questions. Not because she lacked faith, but she was amazed and wanted to know: "'How will this be...since I am a virgin?'" (Luke 1:34). And Zachariah, John the Baptist's father, was downright doubtful, causing him to lose his ability to speak throughout his wife's pregnancy (verses 18-20).

As for Joseph, he remained silent. He was told his wife's body was borrowed to carry God's Child. He could not touch her sexually during their honeymoon period until she gave birth six months later (Matthew 1:25); he was instructed to take this Baby whom he didn't father as his own; and above all, he had to be willing to have his reputation as a *dikaios* butchered. Yet Joseph had nothing to say in revolt. God gave a command, and although it required personal sacrifices; although it dragged him through mud and caused him to suffer; although it handicapped him for the rest of his life; and although he didn't fully understand it, Joseph obeyed. No questions asked, no explanations demanded. The worst part of his ordeal was that Joseph never got the chance to see that his distress had been worthwhile.

Before Christ began His earthly ministry; before He opened the eyes of the blind and restored life to the dead; before He ascended the Cross of Calvary, forever breaking the chain that tethered humanity to the power of evil, and bridged the abyss between heaven and earth; before He rose to glory on the third day, and ascended to heaven in the flesh, this righteous man of God, who gave his best for Christ's incarnation, closed his eyes in death![21] He never got the chance to say, "My work was well worth it!" He never experienced a father's pride when the boy he raised became a man and honored the family name. Joseph died before any of this could happen.

The majority of Christians seek a compliant Savior. They want an easy Christianity, one that suits their need and checks off everything on their list of dos and don'ts. They expect to make their demands and have God obey them, no questions asked.

But what if God said, "Everyone who wants to live a godly life in Christ Jesus will be persecuted" (2 Timothy 3:12)? What if He said, "Many are the afflictions of the righteous" (Psalm 34:19, NKJV)? Or "'we must go through many hardships to enter the kingdom of God'" (Acts 14:22)? Would you still have faith? Would your faith survive if God proposed to take your money? Your health, maybe? Would you still have faith tomorrow if it meant trading the warmth of your bedroom for a cold park bench?

No one will move beyond this earth to inherit glory without faith, and no faith is constructed without pain. If you desire to see God's glory manifested in your life; if you long to be His friend and confidant, to be considered by Him for great assignments and honorable posts, know that this comes at a price.

True faith is not serving God when the blessings pour in. It is not jumping up and down in praise when prayers are answered. True men and women of faith understand that the pathway winding up toward heaven is filled with surprises, inconvenient appointments, dark corners, pitfalls, and ditches. They understand that sometimes the bottom will fall from under them, sending them crashing to the ground with a painful thud.

Nevertheless they move forward! They brave the tempests and boldly face calamities, regardless of the perils to their own lives and regardless of the inconveniences that faith sometimes brings. They know that, in the end, God will reward their faithfulness, even if they must perish in their shame. They praise and celebrate God not just when promotions are received, but also when they are called to be mauled by hungry lions (see Daniel 2:48, 49; 6:10-16).

Raw-deal faith—unfair, no-strings-attached faith—matters to God because He wants man's allegiance out of love. To Him that faith is worth our suffering; it is worth allowing us to endure life's worst-case scenario.

LAST WORDS
The Hall of Faith

THERE is hardly an athlete who would not want to be inducted into the hall of fame someday.

Induction into a hall of fame is the highlight of a sportsman's career. Halls of fame honor the bests, those whose achievements prove noteworthy. Inductees are often enshrined with sculptures, plaques, and memorabilia for breaking old records and setting new ones, for superior performances and breakthrough achievements.

Being inducted into a hall of fame is difficult. Rules and regulations to qualify are stringent. Inductees must distinguish themselves not only in performance and ability but also in sportsmanship, and their presence to their field of endeavor must have resulted in major contributions.

Scripture offers a glimpse of God's Hall of Fame, or rather, His *Hall of Faith*. Far from being a complete list, only sixteen individuals are named.* And what a group it is! As you read the names and think of their impressive résumés, you may be tempted to retreat into a hole, convinced that it is impossible to be inducted into the Hall of Faith. Let's meet the inductees:

Abel: The first martyr, recognized for his incredible faith in God's promised Deliverer.

Enoch: A man who lived so piously, with such holy obedience, and who was so intimate with God that one day the Lord decided to simply take him home to heaven to be with Him.

Noah: Preserver of the human race from the flood and its progenitor afterward, a "preacher of righteousness" (2 Peter 2:5), and a man of deeply rooted faith and obedience.

Abraham: A man of resolute, unshakable, immovable, tried-and-true faith, christened the father of all people of faith (Galatians 3:7).

---

* Although many others are identified by their deeds; see Hebrews 11, KJV.

Sarah: Abraham's wife, who ended up birthing a child at the ripe age of ninety, a time when she was "past age, because she judged him faithful who had promised" (Hebrews 11:11, KJV).

Isaac: Lauded for his faith in blessing Jacob.

Jacob: A man who "'struggled with God and with men" and overcame (Genesis 32:28).

Joseph: A man who with patience and faith endured the yoke of slavery and wrongful imprisonment for thirteen long years, trusting in the God who seemingly thrust him into a miry pit at age seventeen and forgot about him.

Moses: Second to God's Incarnate Son, Moses was possibly the greatest man of faith to ever live.

You are a little discouraged, aren't you? You must be thinking, "If I have to stand in the ranks of those great men and women of God then there is no hope for me." But keep reading, and you will come across inductee Number Ten.

Inductee Number Ten does not fit the mold of a typical person of faith. Number Ten appears to stand alone. Far from being your model believer, this *hall of faither* seems out of place—like the black sheep of the bunch. After reading her name most of us would think, "What is *she* doing here?" And Scripture offers no apology for her, makes no attempt to hide what she was. "By faith Rahab the prostitute..." (Hebrews 11:31).

Rahab the prostitute? In the *Hall of Faith?*

She was a harlot, a lady of the night—someone who engaged in illicit sex for money, who was considered base and unworthy. She was the kind of woman you might see on the street corner dressed in a skimpy outfit, seductively trying to land her next customer—or victim. You would probably avoid all contact with her, as if she had some contagious disease. You might move to the other side of the street or speed up your driving so as not to risk even talking to her.

She was the type of woman whom Scripture warns "reduces you to a loaf of bread, and...preys upon your very life"; "her house is a highway to the grave, leading down to the chambers of death" (Proverbs 6:26; 7:27). Yet here she is, standing next to one of Scripture's greatest men of faith. And if you think *she's* out of place then you ought to read some more.

Right after you pass Gideon and Barak, soldiers of remarkable faith, you will come across another equally broken vessel, a man who is the perfect picture of brokenness—inductee Number Thirteen: Samson. And then, as if nothing ever happened, the list of faith giants continues: Jephthah, David, Samuel....

How do folks like Rahab and Samson make it onto such a list of biblical dignitaries? Better yet, how can people like you and me, broken to the point of becoming crumbs, ever hope to have our names inscribed on that list?

The Bible gives us the condition for election into the Hall of Faith: *faith!* You don't need the credentials of Moses, the wisdom of Solomon, or the patience of Noah to qualify. You don't need Elisha's power or David's boldness or Daniel's intelligence. You need faith—raw, trust-God-no-matter-what faith. The rest will follow. It is faith that makes frail men like Moses and Abraham and former immoral like Rahab and Samson so powerful and bold.

Rahab the prostitute was inducted into the Hall of Faith because she exhibited faith in God—not the dead or bankrupt faith we see in many "Christian" churches today, but a deed-producing, righteousness-rendering faith that compelled her to risk her neck by sheltering and aiding Israel's two spies to escape from Jericho's royal delegation (Joshua 2).

Samson, taking God's grace for granted, squandered his life with prostitutes and in revelries, associating himself all his adult life with people who did nothing but bring him down. Eventually he hit rock bottom, and even that fell from under him. There he stood at the twilight of his life, blind and bound in chains between two posts among a throng of pagan characters. But in the midst of his shame and blindness, Samson had the sense to call upon the God of heaven, whispering the simple words, *Remember me!* Today he, too, is enshrined among Scripture's worthies.

The thief hung on the cross with a life of crime behind him and suffering in his present while imminent death awaited. He had no time to perform faithful deeds, but had just enough time to express with words the faith that had come over him, welling up inside like fire shut up in his bones. Borrowing the words of Samson he, too, prayed, *Remember me!* Recognizing in Jesus the Incarnate Son of God, he put his faith in Him, and was immediately promised access to the Hall of Faith.

Hall of faithers are not perfect people. With the exception of Enoch, if you search diligently enough you will find skeletons in the closets of most of these men and women. You will find a former liar, a doubter, a drunkard, one with low self-esteem, a prostitute, and even a couple of murderers. But grabbing the hand of faith, having allowed God to burn off their dross in the fiery furnace of faith construction, they all emerged as heroes, dignitaries, and worthies.

Vance Havner says, "God uses broken things. It takes broken soil to produce a crop; broken clouds to give rain; broken grains to give bread; broken bread to give strength. It is the broken alabaster box that gives forth perfume—it is Peter, weeping bitterly, who returns with greater power than ever."[22]

God makes use of unreliable, failure-prone human beings like you and me. Our defects and subsequent healing can be used to save somebody else. This is not a cause to celebrate our faults; we must always strive to grow into the image and character of Jesus Christ, with God's help. This is a reminder that God can use us wherever we are while He gradually constructs us. He is not as concerned with how we begin as He is with how we finish. Just ask the thief on the cross.

The cast of characters in Scripture's great *Hall of Faith* shows that God's heroes are chosen not because of their personal endowments or superior human genes, but because of their unwavering faith in Him. So do not give up hope if you look in the mirror and see a Samson or a Rahab staring back at you. Have faith in God, go through the construction process, and let Him do with you as He did with them. You, too, can become a worthy hall of faither.

4

GOD'S 20/20

THE HUMAN EYE is incredible!

It is considerably small, just about one inch in diameter, but it is extremely intricate. This tiny, fluid-filled globe is packed with millions of cells interacting in such amazing ways that, one writer says, it would take a supercomputer more than 100 years to simulate what takes place in an eye in just fractions of a second.

In its most simplistic form, the eye operates like a camera. Diverging light rays enter it via a transparent covering called the cornea and through a small variable orifice at the center of the iris, the colored portion of the eye, known as the pupil. Behind the iris, the lens bends and focuses light onto the retina, which is the light-sensing mechanism deep inside the eye. Inside the retina are sensory cells known as rods and cones.

Rod cells permit the eyes to detect motion, help provide vision in dim light or at night, and control peripheral vision. Cones provide clear, sharp central vision and detect colors and fine details, allowing us to see in bright light. Ultimately these cells produce chemical reactions and form a chemical known as "activated rhodopsin." This photosensitive chemical changes the light into electrical impulses that the optic nerve sends to the brain, and the brain interprets them as images.[23]

FAITH SEES LIFE THROUGH GOD'S LENSES

VISUAL acuity is measured by placing individuals twenty feet from a Snellen eye chart and testing how well they can see its details. Having normal, or 20/20, vision means that you can see what the average person sees standing twenty feet away from the chart. If your vision is 20/10 then it is better than normal, and you can see at twenty feet what a normal person sees standing only ten feet from the chart. The reverse is also true: 20/50 vision means you need to stand twenty feet away to see what the average person sees with as much clarity and details standing at fifty feet. In the United States, you are legally blind if your vision is 20/200 or worse.

There are many conditions that can impede our ability to see. A very common condition is myopia. People with myopia (nearsightedness) are able to see close objects fairly well but have difficulty seeing objects that are far away. This is because the light that enters the eye comes into focus *in front* of the retina. Hyperopia (farsightedness) is the opposite. People with this condition can see distant objects clearly but struggle to see those that are close. Hyperopia occurs when light rays come into focus *behind* the retina. Both of these conditions, and many others, can be corrected with eyeglasses or contact lenses.

The beauty of corrective lenses is that they give you an entirely new perspective on life. The moment you put them on, things around you come into focus. Corrective lenses redirect light rays such that they come into focus on the retina. Your eyeballs are still defective, but as long as the correct lens is in place, it compensates for your eyes' inability to focus light and helps you to see clearly. That's the power of corrective lenses! They remind me of another type of eyewear.

If you look at life with purely human eyes, what you get is a sorry picture. Once during a layover in Miami, Florida, I saw a news story on CNN about two boys, between ten and fifteen years old, who attempted to rob a woman at gunpoint. When the woman explained that she had no money to give them, they shot and killed her sixteen-month-old baby in retaliation.

In societies like ours, with the economic downturns and climate instability of the 21st century, it is easy to view life with pessimism and defeat. Natural disasters claim thousands, sometimes hundreds of thousands of lives every year. Millions die around the world as a result of violent crimes. Malnutrition and wars ravage countries around the planet. Terms like familicide, rape, nuclear proliferation, school shootings, and global warming have become routine in our conversations. With all of these atrocities, not to mention our personal daily struggles to survive, it is easy to fall into depression, to become fearful or bitter, to view God as a stranger to our predicaments. But take a second look, this time with a set of spiritual corrective lenses sitting above the bridge of your nose, and you will see something entirely different.

Faith, like eyeglasses, corrects our vision. It refocuses life's images so we can perceive their spiritual meaning, however dim the perception at times. Just like glasses do not correct our eyes, faith does not necessarily change our circumstances. The world is still chaotic; the picture is still grim. Faith does not even alter the results of bad decisions or foolish behaviors. What it does is enhance our vision such that, when we look at life, we can somehow see past the horrors to behold God's hand at work. It corrects our flawed human perceptions and enables us to see life from God's perspective. It shows us that persecution, pain and affliction can have purpose. Life's worst case scenarios can become tools for ministry and communication channels through which God reaches people whom He otherwise might not.

Jean-Pierre de Caussade spoke well when he said that "A living faith is nothing else than a steadfast pursuit of God through all that disguises, disfigures, demolishes and seeks, so to speak, to abolish him." Living faith provides clarity in our dark moments, switching our focus from ourselves to God, such that we see the world from the vantage point of eternity. What many perceive as great loss we see as potential blessings, because we know that God always has our very best interests at heart. So we take life in stride, accepting the good and the bad as they come, believing that somehow God can and will make all things work out for our benefit. Philip Yancey calls this ambidextrous or "two-handed" faith. He describes it as follows:

> I take 'everything without exception' as God's action in the sense of asking what I can learn from it and praying for God to redeem it by improving me. I take nothing as God's action in the sense of judging God's character, for I have learned to accept my puny status as a creature—which includes a limited point of view that obscures the unseen forces in the present as well as a future known only to God. The skeptic may insist this unfairly lets God off the hook, but perhaps that's what faith is: trusting God's goodness despite any apparent evidence against it. As a soldier trusts his general's orders; better, as a child trusts her loving parent.[24]

FAITH IN THE TRENCHES

THE popular thought, "Every setback is a setup for a comeback," is easy to accept conceptually but difficult to assimilate. Recognizing God's glorious design in the face of adversity is easier professed than practiced.

It does not take much to celebrate when we dwell on the highest point of the city. "God is faithful" rolls easily off the tongue when we are clad in the latest fashion, our job titles are impressive, and our bodies are healthy. But when we are pressed against the ropes, when terminal illness eats away at our bodies and death knocks hard at our doors, honoring God becomes a much bigger challenge.

God sometimes allows us to fall into the trenches in order to make better use of us. But there the confidence of even the most faithful can be shaken, and many formerly devout followers turn their backs on God when waves of adversity throw them into a ditch. Unanswered questions and unheeded petitions lure us into a place of anger and bitterness.

Surprisingly, in the trenches is also where many learn the preciousness of God's love. In the wake of life-altering ordeals, after long bouts with acceptance, some come to view their pains as setbacks that have served as stepping stones for incredible comebacks.

Joni Eareckson Tada is a popular author, public speaker, singer, and painter. She has been featured in conferences around the world, has written several books, starred in a movie about her life, is a bestselling recording artist, and a radio program host. Popular magazines such as *People* and *Time* have written about her. Her reach transcends national borders, and millions have been inspired by her work. But Joni's intimacy with God was forged under the most horrendous circumstances. She is the embodiment of a faith that blossoms in the trenches.

On a fateful day in July 1967 Joni, then a teenager, suffered a severe spinal cord injury that left her paralyzed from the shoulders down, after diving into a shallow body of water. Unable to feel the rest of her body, the former carefree 17-year-old who was obsessed with horses, swimming, and daring physical activities, found herself lying face down, bound to a hospital bed. She could not dress or feed herself or wipe her own nose. She learned that she would never walk again and would have only moderate use of her arms.

The prospect of that kind of life totally devastated Joni. She sank further into despair when she saw her reflection in the mirror. Shocked by the sight of the stranger staring back at her, with a shaved head containing metal clamps on either side, pale skin, and bloodshot eyes, Joni begged friends who visited to assist her in committing suicide—slit her wrists or dump pills down her throat.

Her painful transformation into a woman of faith took about three years. Eventually the bitter questions turned into the pleas of a searching heart longing to know if it was at all possible that God, somewhere out there, could use even her—a quadriplegic. Through contacts with friends and searching the Scriptures, she eventually became convinced that, while there isn't necessarily anything good about her condition, God could nevertheless use it for *her* good, for the benefit of His kingdom, and for the glory of His own name.

Joni's life has been a vivid portrayal of a graceful comeback from affliction. The burning question on my mind and probably on yours is: Does God call all of us to endure such a life? Should each and every one of us look forward to this much adversity as the price for serving God?

Where Do I Fit?

I have long struggled with the question of pain and how God uses it. Every time I read about or meet someone in dire straits, it brings to mind my own mortality, fears, and frailties. Questions ring in my head as to whether I would ever survive life in the trenches if I were to share the lot of the likes of Joni or survivors of atrocities like the Holocaust.

How do you lose everything and praise God in the process? How do you walk the Christian walk with no legs, bound to a wheelchair, depending on others to do everything for you? How do you breathe freely with damaged lungs? Or experience God's peace with a malignant tumor in your brain or cancer cells in your groin?

These are questions that have troubled me. I have to admit that the prospect of suffering, even for God's cause, is not something that I am at all excited about. I dread suffering and death, especially of loved ones, and would much rather walk the pathway to heaven basking in success, having a life of ease, filled with riches and triumphs.

I am also fully aware that such a life would not be the way to glory, because God's Word makes it clear that "'we must go through many hardships to enter the kingdom of God'" (Acts 14:22). So then, what do people like me, who do not welcome pain, do at the prospect of being struck with painful blows as we pursue the path treaded by the Master Sufferer, "A Man of sorrows and acquainted with grief" (Isaiah 53:3, NKJV)?

I believe that God allows adversity to come our way in accordance with the measure of our faith, combined with the role that we are called to play in His grand master plan. He knows the measure of our cup, is fully aware of how much pain we can handle, and would never pour suffering into our lives to the point of overflow. God will never give us pain beyond our ability to endure.

God knew that allowing Joni's accident would refine her, and she would rise from the ashes a star that brightens the way for others to find His kingdom. He knew precisely how much pain she could endure, for how long, where to start and end, whom to put in her life, where she needed to live, and a host of infinite details that may never be revealed to her, that were necessary to forge her into the force that she is today. He would never give me Joni's pain, just as He would not put on Joni Moses' burdens. We each have a certain measure of faith and are wired and programmed in specific ways to play our part in God's grand design.

I like to look at life as a great, multivolume book to which all mankind is called to make a contribution.

Some contribute whole sections to this masterful work. These are impressive individuals who leave their imprint on history in amazing ways, people like the apostles Paul, John, and Peter and King David, Noah, and the great Moses.

There are those among us who contribute chapters, whose global reach is unparalleled. These have brought the gospel to thousands upon thousands and have suffered great pains for Christ.

Some of us contribute pages, others can only provide paragraphs. The beauty of it all is that no matter how small our contribution, it is no less impressive, provided that it uses all that intellect, faith, talents, and opportunities have afforded us.

This work of faith also includes a vast majority who make much smaller contributions—sentences, lines, footnotes, or mere words. Some contribute no more than punctuation. They are like a period that most don't even pause to consider; a comma that the majority of the world overlooks; or a semicolon that people simply don't know what to make of.

But make no mistake: We all contribute something, for better or for worse, and our contributions matter. However small our role is, it is to our own salvation and those of the people around us. The pain we face will be in proportion to our faith and role, and God will make certain that, though it may bring us to our backs, it is never too much to bear. That, my friends, is the mercy of the God we serve.

GOD'S 20/20

YEARS ago *The New York Times* published an article detailing the degree to which prisoners are mistreated in the United States.

The article reported that, in some states, prisoners were stripped bare in front of others and males were forced to wear pink women's underwear as a form of humiliation. The guards beat, verbally abused, and made the prisoners crawl. Some guards allowed gang leaders to buy and sell prisoners as sex slaves. The article also reported that at the time more than 40 U.S. prisons were under court order for poor sanitary conditions, neglect, overpopulation, or abuse.

As awful as some of these treatments sound, they pale in comparison to what Roman prisoners endured in the early first century.

Many prisons in Rome were built underground in deep darkness, and large numbers of inmates were packed into these dungeons like inanimate cargo. The prisons were often cold, food was scarce, and sanitary conditions were deplorable. The chains that shackled the prisoners often caused severe wounds, and since prisoners were neglected, these wounds became infected. As flesh festered and filth accumulated, disease was rampant. The air was fetid, and as "one prisoner of Tiberius remarked...prison food gave no satisfaction but also would not permit one to die."[25] There was constant wailing and roaring among the inmates, and female prisoners had it worst. They were prone to physical abuse and rape by the guards. Suicide was common among both genders.

Paul and Silas were thrown into one such prison in Philippi, a Roman colony, for healing a young slave girl possessed by an evil spirit.

The girl was a cash cow for her masters, meaning she brought them "much profit by fortune-telling" (Acts 16:16, NKJV). People came in groves to consult with her, and paid the girl's masters handsomely for her revelations. As the men made their way to prayer service the possessed girl shouted repeatedly, "'These men are servants of the Most High God, who are telling you the way to be saved'" (Acts 16:17).

Her words, while they expressed truth, were a distraction to Paul's listeners. Perhaps her remarks were sarcastic or referred to God as some nebulous figure that people cling to because they don't know any better, the same way that atheists today refer to a God that they neither know nor respect. According to the Matthew Henry Commentary the girl's remarks were "intended by the evil spirit to dishonor the Gospel. Those who were most likely to receive the apostle's message were those who were prejudiced against these spirits of divination; by this testimony, therefore, they would be prejudiced against the Gospel."[26]

Paul endured her pestering for some time, but eventually got fed up. He healed her in the name of the same Jesus whom she was taunting, making a disciple out of her, and earning for himself and for Silas two seats in one of Rome's worst dungeons (Acts 16:16-24).

The men were stripped naked, their fleshes torn open with lashes, their feet put in stocks, and they were buried in "the inner prison"— that is, in the deepest, darkest hole of the dungeon. I shiver just picturing the scene.

Here were these men of God, good citizens... *scourged and imprisoned for doing good!* The stocks on their feet were instruments of torture so agonizing and left the apostles in such an uncomfortable position that, one writer suggests, sleep was out of the question. Their chains caused wounds to their arms and legs, compounded with lacerations from the flogging. The place was repugnant—it was dark, cold, and reeked of bruised and festering flesh. Voices of the other prisoners, who most likely were criminals guilty of various transgressions, created a cacophony, and the shrieks, moans, and profanity was enough to drive them insane.

Neglected, with blood thickening and crusting around their wounds, these men had every reason to curse God, or at the very least, question His methods. Surprisingly they did the antipode. Instead of complaints they burst out in songs of praise! I imagine their booming basses echoing through the dungeon.

Their singing confused the other prisoners. They were not accustomed to such jubilant, victorious sounds from people in conditions such as theirs. So sweet the singing and so shocked were the other prisoners that they ceased their swearing, moaning, and groaning to listen. The guards couldn't quite understand it either, wondering who Paul and Silas were, and what could possibly prompt their rejoicing while in such abhorrent conditions.[27]

Sometimes the world wonders what's wrong with us. Christians must be from another planet. Maybe they should call us *Martians!* We do peculiar things, believe such nonsense, don't we? After all, Christians think that simply plunging a person into baptismal waters can somehow transform that person into a new creature.

We think a Man could actually walk on water, I mean, how crazy is that!

We believe that some 500-year-old guy got at least one pair of every single land animal in existence to fit into a boat that was about 450 feet long, seventy-five feet wide, and forty-five feet high, and somehow the occupants of that boat survived about one year floating on floodwaters that supposedly inundated the entire planet and destroyed every living organism.

How about this one: We actually believe that all of the marvels of creation—billions of galaxies, universes, star constellations, moons, suns, and countless other bodies that make up the cosmos, most of which we don't even know about—could *really* have been created in six literal, 24-hour, 1,440-minute, 86,400-second days! Can we be so naïve? We definitely have our heads up in the clouds, right?

Wrong!

Christians are certainly not Martians, although I must admit that, to those out of touch with the power that fuels us, we can come across as eccentric, abnormal, a bunch of crazies. And we're proud of those labels, because "God has chosen the foolish things of the world to shame the wise, and God has chosen the weak things of the world to shame the things which are strong" (1 Corinthians 1:27, NASB).

The world does not understand us because it cannot grasp the enormity and limitlessness of the One we serve. Because God is great, He thinks and acts in ways too great for even our understanding. Since we try to emulate Him the world has a hard time keeping up, and because they cannot understand us they dismiss us as lunatics in need of psychiatric treatments. God sometimes bursts onto the scene and proves that our beliefs and ideas are not that foolish after all. He sometimes shows the world that we are not the ones in need of enlightenment.

Seeing Life through God's Lenses

Paul was not always the zealous, fiery apostle we know him to be. Once upon a time, this man had been a staunch defender of the pharisaic sect, a man whose passion for the law led him to extreme limits, to promote the very principles that the law condemned.

Shortly after Christ's resurrection and ascension, His disciples began to teach His principles and build the early Christian church. The Pharisees saw Christ's teachings—His insistence on grace rather than the works of the law and His claims to be the Son of God—as major threats to their traditions and to the wellbeing of the nation. At that time Paul, then known as Saul of Tarsus, was a rising star in the clan of the Pharisees. A Hebrew with Roman citizenship, brilliant and adept in the affairs of the law, he was at the forefront of the assault to extirpate the new doctrine.

Motivated by his fanatical hatred of Christians, Paul used every tool at his disposal to coerce them to abandon their beliefs. He was an accomplice in the death of Stephen, one of the seven deacons chosen by the apostles (Acts 7:58), and he fiercely persecuted the Christian church at large. Paul was "breathing out murderous threats against the Lord's disciples" (Acts 9:1). He was heavily involved in his murderous rampage when Christ thrust him off his high horse (quite literally; see verse 4) and corrected his blinded vision (also literally, verse 18) with a set of faith lenses.

Fast-forward to this point in the story, where we find Paul sitting in prison, praising the Jesus he once persecuted. Cold and hungry, suffering the pain of fresh blows that left his back lacerated, Paul sang exultantly and celebrated the God who is powerful enough to have prevented his circumstances but permitted them anyway. As he praised, something incredible happened.

God dispatched angels to rescue Paul and Silas. An earthquake resulted as the angels stomped their way into the prison, throwing open their heavy bolted doors and causing the chains, fetters, and stocks that bound the prisoners' hands and feet to fall loose.[28] Paul and Silas were set free, and for their sake, so was everyone else in the prison.

There is a reason why Christians today seldom experience wonders like these. Most of us would have gotten stuck on the fact that we are innocent and God's servants. I mean, the man just healed someone of demon possession! Isn't that worthy of recognition? Shouldn't he have been invited as a featured speaker to conferences on how to heal people of demon possession? Shouldn't producers have come knocking, offering Paul his own TV show where he could heal people while millions watched in amazement? Instead he was beaten and thrown in jail.

Most of us would have become bitter. That sleepless night would have been spent moaning like the criminals. We would have looked at our condition through defective human eyes. Paul and Silas looked at theirs through God's lenses, and instead of complaining, they celebrated.

Why?

Because they saw in their scourge a pattern. They recognized that the journey to heaven is not some glamorous affair attended by the elite, where everyone is smiley-faced, sipping exotic beverages, and chatting with society's VIPs about things that make them feel good. The world does not understand us, nor should it. They think we are strange and fanatical—the exact same sentiments they expressed toward Jesus. And look how they treated Him. What makes you think you deserve better treatment?

The prison warden, who was responsible for the prisoners with his life, was as perplexed as the guards and inmates when he fell asleep that night to the tune of Paul and Silas' singing, and got a rude awakening when the earthquake hit. The warden was paralyzed with fear after he rushed to the dungeon and found all the cell doors open. Thinking the prisoners had escaped, and not wanting to endure a humiliating execution at the hands of the Roman authorities, he decided to commit suicide by thrusting himself through with his sword.

But Paul was there. With cheer and a strange mix of love and kindness, Paul cried to the man not to harm himself, assuring him that the prisoners were all accounted for.

Beholding the aftermath of the earthquake, seeing the joy that lived within Paul and Silas, remembering their joyful singing in spite of the horrendous treatment they had received, and realizing that what took place in the prison could only be the result of divine intervention, the jailer threw himself at the mercy of Paul and Silas, desperate to know what he must do to share in their joy.

By the end of the story, not only the jailer, but also his entire family received baptism. We can be certain that the lives of the prisoners and others in the environment were touched as well. Besides, the earthquake was felt not just in the prison but also throughout the region. I can't help but believe that it had dramatic effects on people when they heard the story of what caused it,[29] especially those who had witnessed Paul and Silas' healing of the demon-possessed woman.

There is a lesson here for us.

Sometimes your beating has nothing to do with you. You try your best but still end up suffering…for somebody else's sake. Jeremiah, Hosea, and Paul and Silas are just a few examples of God's faithful servants who endured beatings, imprisonment, attempts on their lives, and adulterous marriages for the sake of other people. I believe that Paul and Silas' imprisonment had more to do with the jailer, his family, and the other prisoners than with Paul and Silas themselves.

Sharing God's visual acuity does not mean you no longer feel the blows when life knocks hard against you. As God's servant you are not exempt from the effects of natural catastrophes; you too feel the pinch of a bad economy and grieve when a loved one dies. What God's 20/20 vision does is change your response. It adjusts your attitude toward pain and suffering, such that even amid the storm, you can see God's hand at work.

Paul's mortal agonies are among some of the worst in Scripture. This is a man whose life was in constant peril. Governors, soldiers, priests, average Joes, and whole cities have at different times stood ready to destroy him. Attempts on his life were a normal occurrence. He had been expelled from cities, repeatedly beaten, and stoned. Here he is in his own words:

"Even now we go hungry and thirsty, and we don't have enough clothes to keep warm. We are often beaten and have no home. We work wearily with our own hands to earn our living. We bless those who curse us. We are patient with those who abuse us. We appeal gently when evil things are said about us. Yet we are treated like the world's garbage, like everybody's trash—right up to the present moment" (1 Corinthians 4:11-13, NLT).

If anybody had reasons to complain and become bitter, it was Paul. Yet the man's theme was constantly one of rejoicing.

"Rejoice in hope of the glory of God" (Romans 5:2, KJV). "We can rejoice, too, when we run into problems and trials" (verse 3, NLT). "Rejoice in our confident hope" (12:12, NLT). "Rejoice with them that do rejoice" (verse 15, KJV). "The Kingdom of God is... of living a life of goodness and peace and joy in the Holy Spirit" (14:17, NLT). "Christ is preached. And because of this I rejoice. Yes, and I will continue to rejoice" (Philippians 1:18). "Rejoice always" (1 Thessalonians 5:16, NKJV). "My brethren, rejoice in the Lord" (Philippians 3:1, KJV). "Rejoice in the Lord always: and again I say, Rejoice" (4:4 KJV).

In spite of all the miseries that he suffered, Paul somehow managed to keep his joy. How did he pull it off?

I believe that what kept Paul going was his ability to see life through the lens of faith, such that when suffering came, he was often able to see God's purpose through it. Even those times when God's purpose was not so plain, when his suffering made no sense at all, Paul still clung to his joy... and to his God. His faith became for him an overflowing pool of joy. Seeing life through the lenses of He who is faithful and true, Paul was able to face circumstances with confidence, for no matter how ominous the threat, it is reduced in significance when seen through the eyes of an omnipotent, omniscient God.

LAST WORDS
Transcendent Faith

EVERY one of God's heroes experienced the raw-deal faith.

Abraham waited twenty-five years for a child he was promised would make him the father of a great nation, only to hear God ask him to kill that very child.

Job was declared "blameless and upright" by God Himself, then buried ten children in one day and sat next to piles of garbage scraping oozing pus from boils that broke out on his body.

God anointed David king of Israel, then let him spend a decade on the run from deranged King Saul, who dispatched assassins to take him out and on two occasions tried to pin him to a wall with spears.

It would take too long to speak of Ezekiel bound by ropes, John the Baptist in prison, Paul the apostle stoned, and many others. God's greatest heroes, His closest friends, seemed to receive the worst treatment at times. Yet for some reason, these guys stubbornly held onto Him. I have a hunch that's why today we praise them as Bible greats. Jeremiah gives one of the best examples of how to view life through the lenses of faith.

Jeremiah was a strong, patient leader who faced enormous occupational hazards yet remained true to his call. He received beating after beating for his faithfulness, and from the most unusual sources. False prophets, kings, priests, friends, family members, and as far as he was concerned, even God Himself attacked and made attempts on his life. The grief he experienced is expressed in powerful and poetic language in the book of Lamentations.

In Lamentations 3 Jeremiah complained that God had broken his bones and walled him in with bitterness and hardship. His troubles were exacerbated when he called for help and the Lord seemed to simply shut the door in his face, turn a deaf ear to his complaints. He weighed him down with chains, walled him in with blocks of stone, riddled him with the arrows of adversity. God broke his teeth and trampled him in the dust. "Like a lion in hiding," Jeremiah grieves, "he dragged me from the path and mangled me and left me without help" (verses 10, 11). Things got so bad that the man forgot what prosperity was.

But how did he respond?

Jeremiah was not naïve; he had not forgotten his plight. "I remember my affliction and my wandering, the bitterness and the gall" he says in verse 19. "I well remember them, and my soul is downcast within me" (verse 20). But Jeremiah decided to look past his affliction and focus on God.

"This I call to mind and therefore I have hope: Because of the Lord's great love we are not consumed, for his compassions never fail. They are new every morning; great is your faithfulness" (Lamentations 3:21-23).

The prophet put on his faith lenses, and was now able to see with unencumbered clarity. The lenses of faith extended his vision beyond the ordinary, allowed him to see past the pain that gnawed at him and focused his attention instead on God's love, compassions, and faithfulness. Commenting on Lamentations 3 one pastor noted that, when God sends us compassions He never sends them in singular form. God sends *compassions* (plural)—a truckload of them. The best part is, He does not reach into yesterday's batch to recycle our blessings. God's compassions "are new every morning." And as he looked beyond God's compassions, Jeremiah noticed something else: he beheld the grandeur of God's faithfulness.

Jeremiah noticed not an okay, or acceptable, or good faithfulness. No. God's faithfulness is great! It is grand, vast, enormous. Jeremiah saw an impressive, distinguished, remarkable, lofty, majestic faithfulness. He further saw God's love, a love that envelopes us such that God's purity does not obliterate us in our sinfulness. It is also the umbrella that prevents our consumption in a perilous world. The prophet took comfort because, through the lenses of faith, he beheld the enormity of God's love, compassions, and faithfulness. The pain had not gone away, but it was now okay, because faith buoyed him beyond himself to see the God of his life.

INTIMACY

5

MUSTARD SEED EFFECT

A S I WRITE this chapter, a wildfire is wreaking havoc across Boulder, Colorado.

Aerial photos of the city declare without words the extent of the damages. Scenic structures and million-dollar homes are reduced to charred ruins. A chimney stands in the ashes where a home once was. Melted glass lies in building wreckage. A cluster of school buses that were once yellow have now turned to grayish black, and sit surrounded by charred trees and the ruins of buildings that were once part of a summer camp.

About 1,000 firefighters from twenty states battled the blaze dubbed "the Fourmile Canyon Fire." The fire, which burned for about one week, covered some ten square miles and caused authorities to evacuate more than 3,000 residents from their homes. It cost in excess of $8 million to contain the fire, which destroyed more than 160 homes—worth about $80 million.

Wildfires are a common occurrence around the world. They range from small brushfires to massive conflagrations that cause extensive damage, and they all begin with a spark: from a lighting strike, a falling rock, a volcanic eruption, or the strike of a match. That spark, sustained by the presence of combustible materials and aided by the weather—strong winds, dry conditions, or high temperatures—can become a powerful inferno that changes direction unexpectedly. It can be so powerful that it jumps gaps such as roads, rivers, and firebreaks, and blaze a path of destruction as it propagates through forests, cities, and villages, destroying trees, property, and human lives.

In spite of their destructive nature, wildfires can have ecological benefits. Their effect on the soil is good for certain plant species that depend on them, as they make the environment more suitable for growth and reproduction. They change the nutrients and temperatures of the soil and release nitrogen and other nutrients into the soil in the form of an ash rich with minerals, and those nutrients become available for the growth of other plants.

The analogy between faith and wildfires is astonishing. They both begin with a spark. Both need fuel to sustain them. Both possess remarkable power and can burn with incredible fierceness. Depending on which side you are standing, the effect of both can be either redemptive or devastating. Equally important, given the right "weather," both can propagate at incredible speeds—resulting in a force that can overrun bounds, a force that nothing in the natural world is able to contain.

FAITH BEGETS FAITH

CONSIDER yourself and God as an aging married couple.

You have been in this marriage since it was new and exciting, have endured the tough times of adjusting to someone new shortly after the honeymoon phase. You have overcome in-laws, major life events such as the births of children, home and car purchases, and sometimes even the deaths of friends and family members. You have supported God, learned about habits and requirements you're not too fond of, and you have celebrated, cried, and fought with Him. Now you reach the point where you *know* Him. Of course you do not know absolutely everything about Him. Besides, He is invisible, all-powerful, and perfect while you are fleshly, weak, and flawed. Nevertheless you know He loves you, has your best interests at heart, and will always do what is for your benefit.

This kind of love goes beyond the initial excitement of having found someone new. It is founded upon knowledge tried and tested, experiences made in the toughest and most enriching of times. You are comfortable in your relationship with Him, not because circumstances are always pleasant, but because you've been around the block with Him a few times, and understand as much as a human being can, that God will make all things—poor health, bad marriage, loss of employment, *all things*—work out for your good.

When you speak about Him you are not speaking of prince charming climbing to the tallest tower of the highest castle to sweep you off your feet; you are speaking of a God who has fought life's toughest battles at your side, who has carried you through the greatest challenges of your life. You are speaking of a God who has earned your trust by promises that have translated into actions, and it shows. People respond to your invitation to God's house because they can tell that you live there. They are convinced that you know Him personally; it shows that you actually benefit from what you claim He can give them.

Pregnant Faith

In John 10:14 Jesus says, "'I am the good shepherd; I know my sheep and my sheep know me.'"

The Greek word for "know" here is *Akouō*, which means "to know in an intimate way." This is the same word that is used when the Bible says, "Adam knew Eve his wife; and she conceived, and bare Cain" (Genesis 4:1, KJV). It is a point of knowing God so intimately that the knowledge causes you to procreate. You know God to such a degree that it produces offspring. The intimacy leads you to engender, not a human child, but a new lifestyle, a brand new character, new attitudes toward life. You know *Him*— not only His voice and requirements, not only the things written about Him, but His character, His philosophy, His very nature. As a result you place explicit confidence in Him, rendering Him unreserved, unquestioned, wholehearted obedience.

Akouō is a mutual knowledge that anchors you to God. It synchronizes your heart and mind with His, to the degree that no matter what someone else could concoct about Christ or how convincing their argument may be, if what is said is out of touch with what you know of His character, you refute it outright. Why? Because you *Akouō* Him—know Him in an intimate way.

This level of maturity with God is what I call pregnant faith. Since you love and trust God and desire so deeply to please Him, your life reflects it. Faith permeates everything that you do. You are smeared over, soaked in faith as it were, to the point where it drips from your clothes. When someone brushes against you in the streets your faith rubs off on that person, and she walks away touched by faith.

Faith produces in us certain deeds, and those deeds become a force that, like the pull of a magnet, draws others toward Christ. Our attitude toward others, the words that proceed from our mouths when reacting to unpleasant external circumstances; these are the things that convict the world. When the world sees how we treat the poor, how genuinely the conditions of our neighbors affect us, how we behave toward those who are cold and mean or whose lifestyles are shameful and indecent, these become in us an overflowing pool of grace for the grace-hungry souls in our surroundings. These are the same attitudes that drew untold thousands to Christ, and they cause our faith to grow and bear fruits in other people.

Mature faith is pregnant faith, and pregnant faith always gives birth. When it does, it brings about more faith. Have a soupçon of faith today and watch it pay dividends. The possibilities are greater and the doors open wider tomorrow. You gain more confidence, more boldness, until faith becomes a way of life.

David was a man after God's heart because of his pregnant faith. It began when he was a shepherd boy in the hill country, grew through his teenage years and his twenties while he was on the run from King Saul, and by his death at age seventy, the man allowed nothing to impose limits on him. True, he had a dysfunctional family and his share of character blemishes, but David never doubted God's ability to do the impossible for him. By trusting the Lord to save him from a fox he gained the confidence to confront a bear. By relying on Him to destroy the bear he grew bold enough to take on a lion. And once God gave him victory over the lion, Goliath was as good as dead.

That's pregnant faith—the kind of faith that begets more faith. Through it Abraham became righteous. By it Moses rained plagues on Egypt and parted the Red Sea. With it Peter had buoyancy over angry waves and gave strength to the crippled limbs of a paralytic. Using it Paul chased demonic forces from a slave girl and raised to life the slumbering boy who fell dead from a three-story building. By that same faith you and I cling to Christ today, and when we exhibit that faith, it begets more faith, both in us and in the world at large.

FAITH BANKRUPTCY

BROTHER L, an older gentleman from my former church, came to me one morning during worship service and asked me to take pictures of the children's choir with his digital camera. I placed the camera on the back of the pew in front of me, and when it was appropriate I reached for it to take the pictures. As I drew out the camera it caught a bulletin, slipped from my hand and fell to the floor, the impact causing the latch on the battery compartment door to break.

I went to Brother L and expressed my regrets for breaking his camera. I offered to replace it, but he said no, I didn't have to. Seeing his disappointment and hearing his complaints that this camera had been a gift from his grandson, I insisted that I'd replace it anyway, and would do so within one month.

From that day forward every time Brother L saw me he would complain and ask: "Where is my camera?" The first time he did this I repeated my original promise to replace the camera in a few weeks. Strangely, that did not stop him from asking me about it again the very next time he saw me, which was probably a couple of days later. After about a week or so dealing with this I became frustrated and decided to break my budget and replace the camera. But first I expressed my frustrations to my wife.

I shouldn't even have to replace the camera, I told her. *I was doing the guy a favor. He came to me! Why is he pestering me, even after I took the initiative to replace the camera?* "I should really give him a piece of my mind!" I said.

"Well, you can't do that," my wife replied.

"And why not?"

Nahum smiled and said, "Because you're a Belony!"

I couldn't argue with that.

Growing up I used to always hear my father say, "We're great!" Dad certainly did not mean that he was better than everyone else. What he meant to say was, because of who he was, there are certain things that he simply would not do.

My father would not engage in petty retributions, never put things above people, would not connive to get ahead, and always made whatever he owned available to anyone in need. This led many so-called friends to take advantage of him. When in anger I would protest and demand that he take action against them, Dad would simply wave them off and say, sometimes even singing it, "We're great! We're great!"

My brother Shad and I have tried to carry on the legacy of that greatness, something that my wife truly embraces. She and I spent a lot of time discussing what it means to be a Belony. What does our name represent? Who are we as a family? What are the things that death or life, poverty or richness, sickness or health would never lead us to deny? Whenever I slip and act against the family values, or stand on the verge of doing something out of character, Nahum often reminds me, "You can't do that; you're a Belony!"

As Christians, we bear a name that is of infinitely greater excellence than my father's "greatness." It is a name God is so passionate about that He established a commandment to preserve its purity. "Thou shalt not take the name of the Lord thy God in vain" (Exodus 20:7, KJV). It "is above every name" (Philippians 2:9), a name before which the knees of the greatest of earth's dignitaries and the knees of angels and demons will someday bow (see verse 10).

We represent the name of Christ, for the word Christian means believer in or follower of Christ. When people see us they see more than just a person; they see a representative of the glorious kingdom of heaven. So when we stop meeting the demands of our faith, essentially declaring faith bankruptcy, the damages caused are not just to us as individuals, but especially to God's name and cause.

Bankruptcy is a process by which an individual or business is legally declared insolvent. The entity, voluntarily or at the demands of its creditors, is adjudged incapable of meeting its debts by a court, and in some cases its assets are divided among creditors. In the case of faith bankruptcy, the process is a lot less dramatic but a lot more damaging, with both immediate and eternal implications.

Many "Christians" waste away their resources and natural prowess. They engage in destructive behaviors and questionable dealings that eat away at their faith and deteriorate their relationship with God until eventually there is nothing left to meet the demands of Christianity. They have no love for their neighbors, no compassion for the suffering, and no desire to see the lost saved. All talents are either buried in the sand or used in ways that exalt self rather than to God. Conscience becomes dull. Faith grows old and wrinkly and, with time, depletes to the point of bankruptcy.

Faith bankruptcy is usually involuntary, and occurs when an individual ceases to remember who he is and Whom he represents. The devil, now the judge and ruler of his life, divides the assets that God has given him among so many creditors—employment, pleasure, hunger for riches and honor, drugs, and a cluster of other addictions—that there is nothing left to invest back into God's cause. His priorities are shifted from the eternal to the temporal, and he develops spiritual myopia—becomes so shortsighted that life is all about here and now.

This is a condition that puts you at odds with God. A faith bankrupt Christian focuses more on church politics than on doctrine. He is more passionate about position than service, prefers to receive than to give. On one extreme he is disengaged, a Christian via remote control; on the other he sees himself as an indispensable ingredient in God's cause, in that nothing is good enough unless it has his seal of approbation. Few things are more damaging to Christianity than a Christian with bankrupt faith. I can think of at least three reasons why faith bankruptcy is so destructive.

1) Faith Bankruptcy Dishonors God

To many on this side of heaven, God is just an idea, just one of the many options for people trying to escape the insanities of life. As true and real as God is, regardless of the fact that they could not draw a breath or take a step without Him, a great number of people on planet earth repudiate God.

So the Lord chooses us Christians to be His ambassadors here on earth. He places His church at the center of it all, to be the embassy of heaven on earth, to teach the world what He is like. Because the world does not know God, they view us as the paradigm for who He is. To get a glimpse of God, they watch us; they listen to our speech to hear His voice; and they judge Him based on what we do. When we have become faith bankrupt, our conduct paints the wrong picture of God.

If we are thieves, then our God must be the biggest thief of them all. After all, *we represent Him.* If we are liars, backbiters, and fornicators; if we beat our wives and avoid paying the government its due in taxes, then our God must be the biggest liar, backbiter, fornicator, wife beater, and tax evader in the universe. People will honor or discredit the God of gods based on *my* actions! That's a sobering thought.

In *Disappointment with God,* Philip Yancey suggests that the holy, perfect God of heaven lives in us to the point where His holiness becomes subject to us. Being part of the body of Christ, our behaviors become God's behavior. "In the age of the Spirit," Yancey writes, "God delegates his reputation, even his essence, to us. We incarnate God in the world; what happens to us happens to him." And "the watching world judges God by those who carry his name."[30]

Francis of Assisi spoke well when he said, "Preach the gospel constantly, and if necessary, use words." D. L. Moody puts it this way: "Of one hundred men, one will read the Bible; the other ninety-nine will read the Christian." What they read in us is what they will believe to have read of God. Our primary gospel preaching should not be done with mere words, but with our deeds—deeds that reflect God's character.

2) Faith Bankruptcy Leads to Un-grace

One April morning, a homeless man lay face down on a sidewalk in front of an apartment building in Queens, New York, bleeding from a knife wound. Apparently the man had tried to help a woman involved in a scuffle with another man, and when he intervened, the other man stabbed him. For about one hour the homeless man lay on the sidewalk as one pedestrian after another passed him by.

Surveillance cameras showed that at least seven people walked by, noticed the pool of blood thickening underneath him, and walked away. Some merely glanced. Others stared. One even went so far as to lift up his body. Eventually every single person who saw him that morning went on their way, until the victim died from his wounds, right there on the sidewalk!

We live in an extremely grace-deficient society. People have become so parsimonious in grace that the greatest need of our neighbor goes unmet, to the point where even a dying victim cannot expect to find help when it is so obvious that he needs it. The sad fact is, as Christians, we often do not provide a better alternative to society's grace scarcity.

One of Christianity's greatest ills is Christians whose grace wells have run dry. Bankrupt of faith, which is the conduit of God's grace, they forget the most fundamental principles of Christianity: loving God and loving one's neighbor as oneself. They develop the syndrome of legalism, whose symptoms include extremism and a fervent obsession with mundanity. Consumed with their own agendas, God's expressed commands take a back seat.

They dismiss the needy, ignore the pleas of the suffering, and censure those in society whose lifestyles prove that they are in direst need of grace. Social injustice, racism, world hunger—these are small issues for them. Instead they spend their days worrying about politics—the next house, senate, or presidential race. They are too busy advocating their conservative agenda before Congress to care about prison inmates, homeless shelter dwellers, and substance abuse victims.

Un-grace is especially dangerous because the grace-deprived seldom understands his deficiency, and fails to realize to what degree it is damaging Christ's image. It is a sad fact, but the folks who flocked most to Jesus when He was on earth are the types who mostly avoid our churches today. That is because our grace-deficiency tends to force people to obey God instead of teaching them to love Him by first extending love to them. Obedience to God's commandments ought to be in response to love. Christ Himself stresses, "*If you love me*, [then] you will obey what I command'" (John 14:15).

Christ first focused on showing people the love of God. Their needs—spiritual, physical, and psychological—always took precedence. Before denouncing sin or preaching the kingdom of heaven, He first healed their sick, fed their hungry, and raised their dead. The greater the need, the more tender His touch. However many faith bankrupt followers today, rather than showing the lost the love of God, instead spend their time shoving the commandments down their throats. They scathingly revile the homosexual and the prostitute and the murderer and the rapist and the child molester. As a result these respond with resentment. Instead of being pulled toward us as they were toward Christ, they leave town at the sight of us!

Philip Yancey laments, "The worse a person felt about herself, the more likely she saw Jesus as a refuge. Has the church lost that gift? Evidently the down-and-out, who flocked to Jesus when He lived on earth, no longer feel welcome among His followers."[31]

Os Guinness was equally sorrowful when he wrote, "In the decades I have followed Jesus, second only to the joy of knowing him has been the sorrow at the condition of those of us today who name ourselves his followers."[32]

Chuck Swindoll suggests that "the church must be a place where words are reliable, worship is meaningful, faith is invincible, grace is noticeable, and love is tangible."[33]

Christ in no wise tolerates sin. He called it out, challenged people who toyed with God's commandments and who attempted to trample them underfoot (see Matthew 23). Nevertheless when faced with the physically, socially, and morally destitute, Christ responded with love, pity, care, grace. If you are His follower, then you are called to do likewise.

3) Faith Bankruptcy Deprives the World of God's Blessings

Peter and John were on their way to the temple for prayer service at around 3 p.m. one day (Acts 3:1). As they approached the temple gate called Beautiful, they saw a group of friends carrying a forty-year-old man to the gate; the friends brought him there every day to scrounge. The crippled beggar saw in Peter and John his next meal ticket, and naturally begged them for a few coins.

A broke Peter responded, "'Look at us!'" When the man looked at him he said, "'Silver or gold I do not have, but what I have I give you. In the name of Jesus Christ of Nazareth, walk!'" (verses 4-6).

Obviously the man was shocked, unsure of how to respond to such a command. I can imagine him wondering, "You mean on *these* legs? Have you seen the legs I was given?" Realizing the man's hesitation, Peter took the crippled man by the hand and he pulled him to his feet. Suddenly the tired old legs, so long useless, felt an incredible sparkle of grace. Christ's power, summoned by Peter's faith and channeled to the man's legs, gave him the ability to walk.

Overjoyed, the man began running and jumping, worshipping God for healing him. "Then he went with them into the temple courts, walking and jumping, and praising God" (verse 8).

Notice initially what the cripple's expectations were—all he wanted were a few coins. Perhaps he didn't expect to receive even those. After all, he must have been used to disappointment and rejection. But because Peter was a man of faith, this formerly crippled man was now healthy and able-bodied. Moreover, not only was he physically healed, he was also won over for Christ, and more than likely, some of those who personally knew him and saw him healed became followers of Christ as well (see verses 9, 10).

Now imagine if Peter had been faith bankrupt.

I can almost hear him wonder aloud when he sees the man: "This man must be crippled because he is a sinner. Either he or his parents are responsible for his current predicament; let him pay the consequences of his own sins." (cf. John 9:1, 2; see also Exodus 20:5). Perhaps Peter would have said, "This man is begging because he's just too lazy to get a job!" Or how about this one: "Get away from me; I'm late for church!"

A faith bankrupt Peter would have been judgmental. He would have been uncaring—indifferent to the crippled man's pain. Instead of seeing his suffering he would have seen the impairment as an opportunity to censure him. The bankrupt disciple would have pitted himself against the crippled man and rejoiced that he was not like this man—he was better (cf. Luke 18:10–12). His faith bankruptcy would have robbed the poor soul of physical as well as spiritual healing.

Your lack of faith hurts those around you.

God has given us His Spirit and, along with Him, incredible power (see Acts 1:8). When activated by faith, the power of God in us can accomplish remarkable feats. Like God's men of old, we can pray for the sick and they will receive healing. Evil spirits don't stand a chance. We can even speak to death, one of humankind's greatest enemies, and it will have no choice but to recede in defeat! God has armed us, His children, with mighty power.

But when we are faith bankrupt, God's power in us becomes

lethargic, lazy, worthless. A worthless faith does no one any good. In fact it causes harm by leading to un-grace. You rob somebody of healing, of comfort, and of protection, and fail miserably of putting a dying soul on the path to heaven—dare I say, you may even send her in the opposite direction—when your faith is bankrupt.

Imagine if Joseph had been faith bankrupt. Things would have gone down differently with Potiphar's wife; Israel and his family would have paid the price as a result. They would have suffered great loss during the famine that struck the whole region (see Genesis 41:54; 42:1–3; 43:1, 2). At a minimum, they would not have enjoyed the generosity that Pharaoh extended them because of Joseph.

What if Elisha had been faith bankrupt? The indebted widow would have lived to see her boys become slaves. The Arameans would have entrapped the Israelite king. And the dead man thrown into his grave would never have had a second chance at life.

Now imagine the blessings you may be depriving someone with your faith bankruptcy!

MUSTARD SEED EFFECT

NAAMAN was a strong, disciplined man, a powerful military leader; the Bible has nothing ill to say about his character. But this great figure, although he apparently retained his position as commander of the Syrian army, had the misfortune of being a leper.

In those days, people plagued with this very devastating disease were deemed cursed by God and thought to be paying the price of their sins. No place was found for them in society. They were driven from the company of "clean" people and compelled to join colonies with other lepers, wear mourning clothes, and cry "Unclean! Unclean!" when they traveled to avoid infecting others.

Medically known as Hansen's disease, leprosy had the tendency to spread and was considered highly contagious. Beginning as "a swelling or a rash or a bright spot" (Leviticus 13:2), the disease progressed to destroy the peripheral nerves, leading to loss of sensation in the eyes, nose, ears, hands, and feet. Leprosy patients would hobble around with infected sores, missing chunks of flesh and sometimes entire limbs. So Naaman was contemplating a life of alienation from friends and family, the possibility of total blindness, and the inevitable, slow destruction of his body. It is no wonder that he acted so swiftly when one of his maids made a declaration that shed a glimmer of hope on his doomed life.

Those were the days when Israel and Syria (or Aram) were engaged in constant skirmishes. At least three such wars are recorded in the closing chapters of the book of First Kings. The first two were won by Israel under King Ahab (1 Kings 20:1–21; 22–43). In the third war, the battle in which King Ahab was killed, King Ben-hadab of Syria prevailed (1 Kings 22:29–37; 2 Chronicles 18:28–34). After that last battle, marauding bands of Syrians constantly raided Israel's borders, and during one such raid, brought back a little Israelite girl who ended up serving the wife of Syria's fearless military commander.

The Seed of Innocent Faith

Since the Bible is silent on the maid's name, to make the story easier to tell, I will call her "Nameless."

Our young friend, Nameless, had become a victim of circumstances. Her life took a drastic turn. One day she was a young child with no real sense of responsibility other than regular household chores, her hair, nails, and keeping up with friends on that era's version of social networking and smartphones, and the next she was a working woman—responsible at least in part for maintaining an entire household. She had to deal with the shock of starting over in a new country, was compelled to adapt to a new culture. And who knows what degree of loss she sustained during that raid.

Perhaps her parents had been killed. Her siblings, if she had any, may have been forced into servitude as well; she doubtless had no hope of ever seeing them again. I imagine she must have had childhood aspirations, but those were now shattered. Her freedom? Lost. Her individuality? Stripped away. She was now just one of many who serve, but thank God she was a child of faith.

Nameless had all the reasons in the world to blame Naaman for her misfortune. For one thing, he was Syrian, and that automatically made him one of the oppressors. Second, she was a servant in his home, doing *his* hard labor. Third, he was a Syrian military commander, someone who possibly exerted some degree of control over the very band of marauders who invaded her homeland and crushed her world to a pulp.

Nevertheless Nameless refused to allow her external circumstances to dictate her internal disposition. She would not become bitter or resentful, refused to allow tribulation to deplete her spiritual resources and render her spiritually insolvent. Unable to change her circumstances, and seeing no immediate solution to her abysmal condition, she firmly resolved to make the best of it. She buckled down, dug her heels in the ground, and stood against the tide of adversity that had come her way. Nameless refused to reward Naaman evil for evil.

Many would have celebrated Naaman's leprosy, drawing the conclusion that his scourge was God's punishment. They would have had no qualms about their desire to watch him squirm, to see him "rot in hell" for all the pain that he had caused. Not Nameless! Instead she desired to see him healed, and ironically, she was the only one who knew how this could come about.

Nameless' response when she heard of Naaman's disease is both innocent and profound. Innocent, because she points out what to her is so obvious that anyone could have thought of it. I imagine she expresses herself as only a young child could. "If my master could get to the prophet in Samaria he would, like, totally be healed of his leprosy" (2 Kings 5:3, paraphrased).

Her response is also profound because it reflects the deep conviction of someone who knows the God of whom she testified. There was no doubt in her mind, no reservations in her heart, no equivocations in her language, no ifs or buts in her attitude. The prophet could do this, she was convinced. He had access to God's power, and with it, could bring healing to leprous Naaman. She only lamented the distance between her master and Elisha.

Perhaps Nameless grew up in a home where honoring God was of primary importance. Perhaps during morning worship her father recounted stories of the prophet's many miracles—how he divided the Jordan, purified water, and raised the Shunammite's son from death. One way or another, this little girl's innocent faith had brought her to the realization that God can do all things, and that His prophet had been endowed with enough power to overcome the most dreadful disease in the world at the time.

How I wish today's Christians had this kind of innocent faith. Instead ours is an unreliable, unstable, to borrow Chuck Swindoll's words, a "wobbly-legged faith."

Nameless had no idea what she had just done. Her words, though simple and innocent, planted in the commanding general the seed of faith, and Naaman absorbed them like a parched ground desperate for a drop of rain. He took immediate action when he heard that there was a power somewhere able to cure leprosy, a power beyond kings, beyond the Syrian gods. He went to his king, the most powerful man in the land, and asked for permission to act upon the words of his powerless slave girl.

Perhaps Nameless had never been acknowledged before. In a book about kings, prophets, and great military generals, we encounter her for only three verses, and just like that, she disappears into the archives of history. Not even her name is mentioned. She had not gained national renown as a foreigner by becoming a statesman like Daniel; she had not shaken the world down to its foundation with great miracles and military conquests; she was not scholarly, perhaps had never even attended school. Hers was an obscure world filled with obstacles and disappointments.

Yet none of these stifled Nameless' faith; she was not pigeonholed by circumstances. Instead she allowed her faith to take flight, and as a result, it made a believer out of Naaman, Naaman's king, his servants, and eventually impacted the whole nation of Syria.

One drop of her faith, planted unwittingly in the heart of the great general, germinated to have mustard seed effect.

Today we too are faced with men and women plagued with leprosy, but of a spiritual nature, and unless drastic measures are taken, they will die from their scourge. Like Nameless, we have the great responsibility to tell them about Jesus Christ, the cure. We don't have to exert great influence over the world or over the people around us. All it takes is to plant the seed of faith.

Notice Nameless did not deliver her message from the mountaintop. It did not come from the pulpit of a "mega church" to tens of thousands of listeners. She did not preach it to millions around the world by way of television or the Internet. She unwittingly preached one of the world's greatest sermons simply by being herself. You and I can do the same.

Risky Business

I believe that faith involves great risks.

Having faith means relying on someone or something else, on their power to uphold honor, their ability to deliver, and on their dignity to behave responsibly with what you have entrusted to them. The fact that you trust means there is a potential for disappointment. Countless have been duped after placing their trust in friends, family members, pastors, political figures, or mechanics. It is even more difficult to trust people that you do not know. Naaman found himself on a slippery slope as he embarked on a journey to seek healing for his leprosy.

Having consulted with King Ben-hadab and gotten his blessings, Naaman made his way to Samaria with a letter from his king to Joram (or Jehoram), the king of Israel. He packed his caravan with 6,000 shekels of gold—about 150 pounds worth. By today's standards, based on actual gold prices of roughly $1,362 per Troy ounce, that pile of gold would be worth about $3 million! And that's not all Naaman brought. He also had 748 pounds of silver and "ten sets of clothing" (2 Kings 5:5). But things got hairy when he arrived in Samaria.

King Joram went into panic mode. He saw Ben-hadab's command—"'With this letter I am sending my servant Naaman to you so that you may cure him of his leprosy'"—as an attempt to pick a fight. Remember, in those days Israel and Syria were constantly fighting, and at this point in history the Syrians had the stronger army. So as far as Joram was concerned this was just a sly attempt on Ben-hadab's part to find an excuse to shed more Israelite blood. His response shows his utter agony.

He tore his outer garment, then expressed his predicament with these words: "'Am I God? Can I kill and bring back to life? Why does this fellow send someone to me to be cured of his leprosy? See how he is trying to pick a quarrel with me!'" (verse 7).

Naaman went the wrong way and could have ended up sorely disappointed. He went to the king of Israel when Nameless was crystal clear that "the prophet who is in Samaria" was the one who could heal his leprosy. Had he not been redirected to the prophet Elisha, not only would his visit have been in vain, but it might have also led to further conflicts between the two kingdoms.

Somehow Elisha got wind of the Syrian general's visit and asked that Naaman be sent to his home. Then came the real test for Naaman.

The powerful military leader came to Samaria with his own pre-conceived notion of how healing should be administered. We do that to God often, don't we? We decide who He ought to be, how He should act, what His response needs to be to our personal trials. God must submit to our examinations before we can declare Him God.

In his position Naaman was used to dealing with dignitaries. He stood in the presence of his own King Ben-hadab and his princes, and must have shared the company of other kings with whom his master interacted (see 1 Kings 20:1). The prominent military leader must have waited in the back of his chariot—I suppose the ancient version of the limousine—outside of Elisha's humble home with his bodyguards, and perhaps some close friends, colleagues, and family members who had come to support him. But the prophet did not even bother to come out to greet him. Elisha simply sent Naaman a message saying (my translation), "Go take seven baths in the Jordan River! That'll do."

I can imagine smoke coming out of Naaman's ears and fire blazing from his nostrils.

He was outraged that Elisha would give him such a simple com-mand. The man expected a parade; he wanted to be treated like the celebrity he was. Naaman wanted to be humored, pampered, and catered to in the healing process. Where was the red carpet? Listen to his complaints.

"'I thought that he would surely come out to me and stand and call on the name of the Lord his God, wave his hand over the spot and cure me of my leprosy!'" (2 Kings 5:11). "Why can't this man treat me like the important figure that I am? Why can't he come out here and humble himself before me, command his God to come down to personally attend to me?"

Naaman's second complaint further highlights the extent of his pride. In addition to demanding that the prophet treat him as the all-too-important figure he perceived himself to be, he went further by proposing an alternative to Elisha's command. He retorted that the rivers in his city, Damascus, were more qualified to heal him than the simple Jordan River of Israel.

I believe that Naaman was enraged for at least four reasons: 1) He humiliated himself by acting upon the suggestions of a little slave girl. 2) He had been turned away by the king of Israel. 3) Elisha didn't even honor him with his presence but sent a servant to speak with him. 4) The prophet told him to go wash, implying he was dirty. It is said that, during that period in history, the water of the Jordan River was not clean but was rather of a brownish green color. So not only did the prophet tell Naaman to go wash, he ordered him to do so *seven times* in a dirty body of water.

That was more than Naaman could bear.

Naaman's pride nearly sank him. A man of his caliber expected the operation that brought him healing to demand a hefty price. And he came prepared to pay, having lugged some $3 million worth of gold to Samaria with him. And when Elisha's command turned out to be so simple—no huge bills attached, no complex medical examinations, no paperwork to fill out or contract to sign—and so humbling—go take seven baths!—he felt humiliated and was ready to abandon ship.

God knew all too well that Naaman's real problem was not leprosy—it was pride. And without a doubt He wanted to teach him a lesson in humility. God taught Naaman that no one deserves special privileges with Him. In the end the great military leader learned many valuable lessons, including this one: obedience to God always makes sense!

Obedience Makes Sense

In his volume on the life of Moses, Chuck Swindoll writes about "the bottom line of cross-cultural ministry or any enterprise of God: Hearing what He says, respecting His call, responding in obedience, and leaving the results with Him."[34]

Faith begins with obedience. Those of us who respond affirmatively to Christ's call do not necessarily do so because of some deep faith that moves us; our first response is an act of obedience. Look back at the calls of Christ's first disciples. All were busy with life when Jesus found them. "Follow Me" He said, and one by one the men obeyed. There was no deep affirmation of faith, no in-depth analysis of His sermons. Obedience came because Christ called.

Quoting Dietrich Bonhoeffer, Os Guinness writes, "'The response of the disciples is an act of obedience, not a confession of faith in Jesus.'" We are not told whether the disciples had ever heard any of Christ's sermons. What we do know is "they did not consider his claims, make up their minds, and then decide whether to follow—they simply heard and obeyed."[35]

God does not believe in instant maturity. Rather than snapping His omnipotent fingers and make us all model Christians, or downloading His Christian upgrade software program into our hearts and within minutes get us ready to enter the pearly gates, God takes His time forming a relationship with us. That requires patience on His part, and from us, obedience. With time, obedience leads to greater knowledge of God, which leads to greater faith, until the point where we can trust Him in spite of seeming contradictions. Take, for example, God's charge to Abraham to kill his son Isaac on Mount Moriah.

This was the same God who, generations before, cursed Cain for killing his brother Abel. Centuries later He would appear to the Israelites on Mount Sinai and declare, "Thou shall not kill!" Yet here He was, commanding a man of faith to kill, not a stranger, but his own flesh and blood.

Obedience to God sometimes challenges who you are. He demands things that can make you scratch your head and wonder whether it is really Him speaking. Nevertheless, you must obey, because in the end you will discover that obedience to God always makes sense.

Naaman faced the ultimate test of obedience. It all came down to what he did at this particular moment. True, he believed his young maid, acted upon that belief by making the journey to Samaria. But there remained one more action—the crucial one—for Naaman to obtain the healing he so desperately desired. And it came at a price. The gulf between scourge and restoration was the willingness to remove the blindfold of his pride, breach the impediment of his obstinacy, and obey. And Naaman nearly failed the test. Thankfully, God often makes it hard for a man not to obey.

On the way back to Damascus, Naaman found himself passing by the Jordan River, at which point his servants and attendants spoke some sense into him. "If the doctor recommended complex medical examinations or major surgical procedures that would cost three million green ones, would you not have gone through them? Then why not just take the baths, man!" To his credit Naaman obeyed, and after the seven baths, walked out of the river a new man, flesh transformed from the rottenness of leprosy to the newness of a baby's bottom.

Planes obey pilots. Musicians obey bandleaders or orchestra conductors. Cars obey drivers. Sheep obey shepherds. Even mules obey their masters. But man refuses to obey his life's conductor. He fusses with God, professes to know better than He, and earns for himself a lifetime of heartaches and pain.

God would teach Naaman humility and obedience, and He used very humble sources to drive home the message: the slave girl, Elisha's servant, and Naaman's own servants. Furthermore,

He caused the proud general to undress in front of all the people present, and everyone saw his leprosy. He went further than that, making Naaman dip himself into a dirty body of water, and do so not once, not twice, but *seven* times.

There was no magic potion in the Jordan River, nor was healing associated with the number seven. Elisha could have said "climb a tree ten times!" and Naaman would have found healing if he obeyed. Obedience was key, and it still is today.

LAST WORDS
God Honors Our Obedience

FROM MY JOURNAL: OCTOBER 2007

We had a choice to make, Nahum and I: pay rent or pay our tithes and offerings.

This was obviously a difficult choice. Not paying the rent would mean many things, especially since we were already a month behind. For one thing, an additional fifty-dollar late fee would be assessed. Second, if this persisted, the landlord might not renew our lease the following year. We could end up being sued. Or worse, we could be evicted. Nevertheless, we decided to ignore all of those threats and pay our tithes and offerings.

We were neck deep in debt during that period in our lives, owing tens of thousands of dollars in credit card debt and college loans. So when we decided to obey God's command we knew what was at stake. And just as expected, the creditors came knocking. They threatened to turn us over to the rude and bullying collection agents if we didn't pay up right away. For about ten days we waited impatiently and prayed, and on October 15, 2007, something incredibly peculiar happened.

I went to the mailbox and found a check in the amount of $578.23! What's incredible is the source of the money. Remember I said we were deep in debt? We owed one such creditor a little more than $5,000, and that bank sent us the check with a long letter of apology detailing how they had overcharged our credit card. Reading the letter, and knowing the history of the debt, I could not fathom how they overcharged us. Here is what I believe happened.

I believe God rewarded our trust in Him. We tithed and paid offerings instead of our rent, and God rewarded our simple faith. It is my conviction that He manipulated the creditor's database to give us the additional money we needed to pay our rent. Or, perhaps, He allowed them to overcharge us, knowing we would believe, and set up circumstances such that the money would come at the very moment that it was needed.

Some would call my conclusion foolish, but then these would be people who have never had such experiences with God. God always honors our obedience. Our act of faith may seem insignificant at times. What God commands may be quite routine, but you never know what great rewards may ensue from simply submitting to "Thus says the Lord!"

"You never know what wonders and miracles will result from simple obedience. Saying yes to God and moving out in faith at His command has an incalculable impact on both time and eternity."[36]

6

THE SCANDAL OF GRACE

THE DAY FINALLY came after months of speculations and threats.

A small nondenominational church in Florida, USA, held what it dubbed "International Judge the Koran Day," in which the church held a mock trial of the Muslim book. According to news reports, the church's pastor presided over the trial, which followed the pattern of legal proceedings in the United States. A former Egyptian Muslim-turned-Christian served as the prosecutor, a current Muslim from Sudan served as the defense attorney, and ex-Muslims and Christians served as "expert witnesses" to help build the case that the book needed to die.

Following the five-hour sham, a jury of twelve Christians found the book guilty of four charges, according to the church's website: 1) "The training and promoting of terrorist activities around the world." 2) "The death, rape, and torture of people worldwide whose only crime is 'not being of Islamic faith.'" 3) "Crimes against women, against minorities, against Christians," and 4) "The promoting of prejudice and racism against anyone who is not a Moslem." The final verdict was execution by one of four means: drowning, shredding, firing squad, or burning. The decision, purportedly reached by an "international poll," was to burn the Qur'an. The book was then soaked in kerosene and set ablaze.

As you can imagine, news of the event outraged the world's 1.5 billion Muslims. Violent protests erupted across several cities in Afghanistan, leading to nearly two dozen deaths and more than 140 injuries. The church's pastor defended his actions, citing Muslim intolerance and violence of Islamic extremists as justification.

This familiar question has become a cliché, but it is appropriate here: "What would Jesus do?"

Throughout His life and ministry, Christ was known for His compassion and love. He felt for people and spent His entire life in ministry to them. From His birth in the slums of Judea to His death for a whole race of undeserving infidels; from His association with the downtrodden of society to His forgiveness of some of the planet's worst offenders, God in the flesh lived and breathed compassion.

Unfortunately, His followers have other priorities. Busy with their lists of dos and don'ts and their specific formulas for earning their way into heaven, they too often forget to obey the greatest commandment next to loving God: loving one's neighbor as one-self. Where Christ was concerned and compassionate, they are condescending and judgmental. Where He showed tolerance, they show bigotry. Where He dispensed grace, they give un-grace.

Of course un-grace is a symptom that points to a much bigger issue. The root cause of the problem is a lack of faith—it is faith bankruptcy. The man or woman who has become intimate with God through faith expresses such faith, not just vertically, but also laterally. A solid faith in Christ, a strong connection with God, must produce care and concern toward those for whom Christ had so much love. Faith in Him must breed compassion.

FAITH BREEDS COMPASSION

GRACE is defined as elegance of form, manner, or motion, something that is attractive and smooth in movement. The word radiates beauty. It represents what is pleasing to the senses, what is exquisite and refined.

Grace also refers to what is charming and cool. The fictional British spy Agent 007, for example (at least the older versions of 007), is considered a man of abundant grace. He is suave, stylish, endowed with certain ability and dexterity. The man defines cool. His speech, his mannerisms, his movements, his gadgets—everything about Bond, James Bond, reveals a man full of grace.

Consider our best athletes. Their mastery of their craft and consistency of performance circle back to one word: grace. We employ grace for the folks that we idolize in our culture, those who appeal to us on account of their beauty, charisma, or accomplishments. It is a form of address to people of royalty, such as dukes and duchesses: we call them "Your Grace." Our celebrities and high-ranking officials bestow great honors upon us when they "grace" us with their presence.

But God's grace reaches higher and is far greater than anything the world could ever imagine.

When Grace Happens

You were caught in the very act, your face plastered over the security TV screens. Your fingerprints have been lifted off the murder weapon; all of the witnesses identify you as the culprit. The evidence presented and filed in court proves beyond the shadow of a doubt that you did the deed—you are guilty as sin, well deserving of execution.

During the trial, having seen and heard the evidence, the jury returned a "guilty" verdict within minutes of deliberation. You can't help it—sin is part of your DNA. And since you are perverted and cruel, justice demands the full penalty of the law: the death penalty. But what did you receive from God?

Rather than sending you to the gas chamber, God walked into the chamber Himself in the Person of Jesus Christ. Meanwhile He offers you a seat next to Him on His throne. You went from condemned criminal on death row to prince with God, even though you are still culpable, still deserving of death. When the verdict should have been "guilty" and the punishment "eternal damnation," God pronounced you "redeemed" and offered "eternal life," leaving you astounded, wondering, *What just happened?* In Max Lucado's words, "Grace happened."[37]

Here is grace in a nutshell: God giving us what we did not deserve and could never earn. Not one of us can tuck our thumbs under our suspenders and strut around telling God how great we are, how deserving we are of His favors. More than 7.4 billion souls populate this small corner of our solar system, and untold billions have passed through earth in centuries past. We have had some truly remarkable characters, men and women so self-denying, so powerful in words and deeds that we hold them in the highest regards.

Yet none of these can point to their résumés to prove to God that they have earned the right to His favors. Every last one of us stands in desperate need of God's grace.

Philip Yancey writes, "Before God we all stand on level ground: murderers and temper-throwers, adulterers and lusters, thieves and coveters. We are all desperate, and that is in fact the only state appropriate to a human being who wants to know God. Having fallen from the absolute Ideal, we have nowhere to land but in the safety net of absolute grace."[38]

Here is Chuck Swindoll in his book *The Grace Awakening:*

"We were born wrong with God. The same sin that Adam introduced has polluted the entire human race. No one is immune to the sin disease. And no human accomplishment can erase the internal stain that separates us from God. Because Adam sinned, all have sinned. This leads to one conclusion: We all need help. We need forgiveness. We need a Savior."[39] Simply put, we all need grace.

The beauty of grace is that, the deeper we are in our mess, the more powerful it becomes. The more desperate our spiritual condition, the more ripe we are for the sweet exchange of grace. It does not matter how far you have plunged, how deep your wound, how low you have fallen, how out of reach you may be to any rescue team, to any other force in the entire cosmos. God's grace plunges to that lowest part and reaches you even there! "How is that possible?" you may ask. It is possible because through grace, in order to rescue us, God needed to come lower than any of us could ever stoop.

"Grace is a God who stoops," Max Lucado writes. "Low enough to sleep in a manger, work in a carpentry shop, sleep in a fishing boat. Low enough to rub shoulders with crooks and lepers. Low enough to be spat upon, slapped, nailed, and speared. Low. Low enough to be buried."[40] Grace comes to us, happens to us, because God stooped very low. And because of His stooping, grace can reach us even when we've plummeted to the very nadir of sin and unrighteousness.

"You have learned that we cannot fall out of range of God's grace. No matter how low we plunge, God's grace goes lower still. The beauty of grace is that it does not leave us there."[41]

That last sentence from Yancey is key. It is not enough for grace to reach us where we are. When grace finds us, it does not simply give us a pat on the shoulder and say, "There you are, I've found you; you're alright now." No! Grace pulls us out, soaks us into the cleansing pool of Christ's blood, and transforms us into the image of God. We walk away as new souls, as people who've received grace transplants. Here is Lucado again:

"Grace is God as heart surgeon, cracking open your chest,

removing your heart—poisoned as it is with pride and pain—and replacing it with his own. Rather than tell you to change, he creates the change. Do you clean up so he can accept you? No, he accepts you and begins cleaning you up. His dream isn't just to get you into heaven but to get heaven into you."[42]

When grace happens, Christ is glorified, and lives are changed. Murderers become apostles. Hard-as-rock hearts become soft and obedient to God's voice. As Swindoll puts it, grace changes not only our hearts but also our faces. We become repositories of such grace. A grace-filled Christian carries grace around with him or her in the office, in the classroom, on the bus, or on the train. We are smeared with it, and it gives off a whiff of grace to anyone we brush against. As Christians, stewards of God's grace, that grace comes with certain expectations.

GRACE EXPECTATIONS

IF you are a child of God and bear the name of Christ, then you are expected to be a dispenser of Christ's grace. The hungry, the thirsty, the lost, the immoral, the dirty and the clean, the haves and the have-nots—all people, of all races, of all walks of life, ought to see Christ's image in you, receive His grace through you.

In a world marred by oppression and greed, violent extremism and wars, where the strong stomp the weak to the dust and the powerful squeeze the powerless—a world of survival-of-the-fittest, dog-eats-dog—grace is desperately and utterly in short supply.

People are hurting. They hunger and thirst not just for food and water but for acceptance, for understanding, for guidance—for grace. Folks need to know that there is something better out there for them, someone who accepts them in spite of their mistakes, in spite of their inconsistencies, in spite of their unlovable characters and personalities. Christ offered the world this much: love, acceptance, and salvation. As Christians, you and I are the ones He has chosen to represent Him, so our job is to help the world feel Christ's presence, hear His voice, see His face.

"We who follow Jesus are called to be dispensers of God's grace, setting loose this powerful force on a weary, violent planet. May the church be known as a place where grace flows on tap: to sinners, to rich and poor alike, to those who need more light, to outcasts, to those who disagree, to oppressed and oppressors both."[43]

When our faith in God reaches the point of intimacy, and Christ's character and image is being formed in us, then we learn to desire the things Christ desires and to see the world the way He sees it. Faith aligns our will with God's to such a degree that His passion for people and their needs becomes ours. Pleasing Him becomes our daily aim, and Christ is pleased when His children show concern for those who are atop His priority list: the poor, the marginalized, the sinner. While the world honors the top performers and the self-sufficient, Jesus caters more to the underperformer, the self-doubter—all of society's neediest members.

As bearers of Christ's name, we are not expected to wield the Bible like a sword, cutting and slashing all those we feel do not measure up to our expectations. Instead we ought to show love, compassion, and understanding. Even when we must be the voice of stern rebuke, when we must cut others through with the truth, let our message be oiled and sweetened with the fine relish of grace.

This grace expectation stems from the fact that we, too, were once (and in many cases still are) as guilty as the ones whom we castigate. It was through the down pouring of God's recurring, life-enriching grace, obtained through faith alone, that we received the antithesis of what we deserved. And God expects that grace to be extended to others.

"The grace the Lord pours into each life is intended for everyone, the whole world. Once it fills His chosen vessel, it should overflow and then flood everything around him or her. That is why He leaves His beloved sons and daughters in the world, to give grace a horizontal dimension."[44]

You don't receive grace and then pinch it as you do your pennies, horde the grace of God for yourself and no one else. Grace ought to be feasted on with others. It is meant to be donated, lavishly dispensed on the people around us. Those who receive grace and keep it to themselves might as well have taken that grace and set it on fire, or buried it in the sand, because "grace received but not expressed is dead grace."[45]

THE SCANDAL OF GRACE

SHE was caught red-handed.

Her accusers had been lurking in the dark, waiting for hours for the right moment to nail her. Their patience paid off. While she was engaged in her illicit act—naked in bed with a man to whom she was not married—the officials burst unexpectedly into her boudoir, grabbed her, and dragged her from under the crumpled bed sheets and onto the streets.

Shamed, humiliated, and exposed, she was taken directly to the temple where the religious leaders who apprehended her— some of whom were no doubt former customers—knew Christ was teaching. The Gospel writer does not hide the fact that the men— rabbis, priests and scribes, whom in our day we would refer to as pastors, elders and deacons—were less interested in the woman's actions themselves than in finding grounds for accusing Christ. No matter how He handled this one, they thought, He'd end up in hot water. Listen to their question:

"'Teacher, this woman was caught in the act of adultery. In the

Law Moses commanded us to stone such women. Now what do you say?'" (John 8:4, 5).

The law said "death by stoning," but Rome, Israel's occupiers at the time of Jesus, said "only our justice system can condemn someone to death." By bringing the case to Christ and asking, in effect, "To whom should we listen, the Law or Rome?" the religious leaders were sure they would have grounds to condemn Him. If He said release her, He would be ignoring the Law of Moses and would be condemned by the people. If He said stone her, He would be assuming authority reserved only for Rome and would be condemned before the Romans. No matter what Christ said, they were sure, they'd *get* Him!

It is worth noting here that these men cut a few corners in order to set their trap. First, the act involved two parties; where was the man? Perhaps he, too, was part of the setup, and joined the crowd, stones in hand, ready to murder the poor woman? Second, the stipulations of the law were such that, both parties—man and woman—were to receive the same fate (Deuteronomy 22:23, 24).

While the men impatiently waited with rocks in their hands to stone the woman, Jesus simply stooped down and began writing. There, in the dust of the temple court, the Lord of Life wrote for the very last time in Scripture. On that canvas of sand, where feet and wind and rain could erase them, Christ enumerated one by one the sins of the religious elite.

I imagine in our day He would write, "Pastor John is sleeping with First Elder Jeff's wife." "Deacon William committed tax fraud." "Elder Matt is secretly a homosexual." You would have heard revelations like insurance fraud, murderer, having an affair with the church clerk, stealing from the treasury, watching pornography, sexual promiscuity, prostitution, stealing from employer, killing with the tongue, etc.

An inspired writer claims that, as the men began to press Jesus for an answer and came closer to drive home their case, their eyes met the pavement where their own secret sins were inscribed for all to see. Overpowered by shame, their countenances changed immediately, as each one was able to read his own transgression, transgressions which the crowd, having noticed the leaders' change in expression, moved closer to see.[46] At that moment Jesus launched His challenge: "He that is without sin among you, let him first cast a stone at her" (John 8:7, KJV). After dropping the bomb, Christ went back to the dust to write down more shameful secret sins.

As you can imagine, heavy rocks began to fall to the ground, and footsteps shuffled away. The woman found herself alone, kneeling before Christ. Though He is the Author of the law that she had transgressed, He saw no need to bring upon her any unnecessary shame. Without a doubt the woman expected Christ's censure—a few harsh words here, a reprimand there; at the very least, tell her what a disappointment she had been, how much shame she had brought upon herself by her disgraceful, immoral actions. She was doubtless used to those kinds of verbal blows.

But Christ did not meet her with a deep frown or harsh words. He reached out and touched her, lavished His love upon her. Instead of censure, Christ gave her grace.

"'Woman, where are those accusers of yours? Has no one condemned you?'" At this point I can see her glance over her shoulders, to her left and right, making sure the angry mob had dispersed, then look up at Him and say, probably through tears, "'No one, Lord!'" So the Lord said, "'Neither do I condemn you; go and sin no more'" (John 8:10, 11, NKJV).

The Shock of God's Grace

We are all too familiar with scandals. It seems as though every institution is fraught with them. From political scandals to scandals in businesses and churches, we see and hear of so many scandals that they cease to surprise us. They become fodder for the media and tabloid news; people make a living tracking scandals. Watching somebody's life in ruins becomes a form of entertainment—we read about it in magazines and blogs, listen to it on the radio, and watch it unfold on television shows. Indeed, scandals are the norm in our society.

Grace is so shocking a scandal because it breaks the law of conventional wisdom. You expect someone who commits a crime to not only get punished but to also receive the scorn of society: the censure of those in authority, the ugly stares of passersby, the murmur of former friends, the rejection of colleagues, the ridicule of media outlets. You expect even family members to feel uneasy and distance themselves, the church to take disciplinary measures and disfellowship the sinful member. Yet that is not what grace typically does.

When Satan drags a reluctant, kicking and screaming sinner before Christ; when he demands our lives as he points to our garments that are soiled with the stains of our indiscretions and reeked with the stink of our sins, Christ, who knows only too well the minute details of our transgressions, and who from the foundation of the world had already chosen to give up His very life in exchange for ours, instead of heaping punishment upon us, rebukes and shames the adversary.

The reality is that Satan's accusations of us are often true. We know that lying is the devil's native tongue—he speaks untruthfulness—but if truth be told, we are *all* guilty of some sin. When he points to our failures, there is often evidence of unrighteousness. This man did in fact steal from his employer; it is true, he committed murder. The woman actually did wreck her family when she left her husband for the smooth-talking executive. Christ sees all of this when He looks at you and me.

But look at the picture in your mind's eye as the accuser makes his case. Christ stops him dead in his tracks. "The Lord rebuke you, Satan! The Lord, who had chosen [put your name inside these brackets], rebuke you!" (Zechariah 3:2). And as if to further shame Satan for even pointing out our defects, God bestows upon us underserving honors. No finger pointing, no rebuke, no reproach. Instead He orders our filth and disgrace expunged, throws the cloak of His grace over our shoulders, and wraps us in the purity of His righteousness.

The Prodigal Son gets no censure; instead he is thrown a party after squandering half the family's fortune. David gets no death sentence, no jail time; he keeps his job as king and even gets his successor to the throne out of the affair with Bathsheba, although his crime and shameful conduct cost Uriah not only his marriage but also his life. You and I exploit God's grace time and again and still live to do so another day. If grace is not scandalous, I don't know what is.

Yet never make the mistake of thinking that grace is cheap. To the contrary, it is extremely costly. God can "get away" with grace because He lavishes it on us at His own expense. Grace is "on the house"—God's house.

When we transgress God's "perfect law of liberty" (James 1:25, KJV), which is a reflection of God's character, the standard of righteous living, we stand condemned under the pressure of the law (1 John 3:4). As a result, the law demands our lives. Since the law cannot be modified—the heavenly Congress cannot simply introduce a bill to amend it to satisfy our fallen state—the natural outcome of sin is our ultimate demise. Remember, "the wages of sin is death" (Romans 6:23).

However something in God, something to do with His love for us, refuses to allow us to die. This presents a dilemma because, since sin was committed, *somebody* needs to die; blood must be shed. And if not ours, the transgressors, then we need a substitute. Because the law is as sacred as God Himself, satisfying its demand for blood requires that the one whose life essence is shed be as sacred as God Himself.

That's where Jesus comes in. God extends us His mercy and grace by taking the full measure of His wrath and placing it upon Himself in the Person of His Son. That is the price of grace—God dying so you and I can live.

I imagine the woman waited on her knees for a few moments, shocked to her very core. She couldn't believe it. One moment she was on death row, heading to the slaughter with an angry mob in pursuit ready for a stoning. The next she was alone with Jesus, humiliated but saved; sinful but not censured; guilty but exonerated. There she was, in the presence of the only One qualified to rightfully pronounce her guilty. Instead the Savior said, "I will not condemn you! Go, you are free. You have been a recipient of amazing grace."

God's grace is indeed amazing, and it is still shocking people today. It is offered free of charge to all who are thirsty, all who are hungry for a life that matters to God. Our past presents no hindrance; our present is no limitation. God liberally offers us His astounding, all encompassing, scandalous grace.

Counterfeit Grace

The very nature of grace makes it an easy target for abuse. The fact that God is compassionate, slow to anger and abounding in love, lures many to go on sinning with the intention of coming back to Him for forgiveness. Grace becomes a spiritual all-you-can-eat buffet line where people can expect to find a continual supply to absorb their spiritually reckless living, and so use it as freedom to sin. That leads to a bogus imitation of grace that many mistake for the real thing.

There would be nothing to stop a pedophile from victimizing a child if he knew the judge would simply let him loose once he said he was *very* sorry. Nor would a murderer reconsider taking a life if he knew he could get away with a simple apology. Why would an adulterous husband deprive himself of the pleasure of a passionate night with a sexy, mysterious woman if he knew his wife would forgive, forget, and stay with him? Grace's nature places it in an alarming position, and many offenders take advantage of it simply because they can.

However freely committing sin because God freely forgives is nothing less than grace abuse—making abnormal, harmful, or improper use of God's grace. That results in a phony version of grace that Christians must reject. I can think of at least three reasons why God's children should work their hardest to avoid the trap of counterfeit grace.

First, you are saved by grace to be like Christ.

Paul, in his letter to the Colossians, illustrates the death of the Christian to transgressions and his renewed birth in Christ by way of His resurrection. You were "buried with him in baptism and raised with him through your faith in the power of God" he writes (Colossians 2:12). "When you were dead in your sins and in the uncircumcision of your sinful nature, God made you alive with Christ" (verse 13). In chapter 3, he admonishes those alive with Christ to live like it.

Since we are now members of God's family, "raised with Christ" our hearts—our inner beings, the seat of our deepest emotions—ought to be set "on things above, where Christ is." And our minds—our power of reason, our faculty for discerning right from wrong—ought also to be set "on things above, not on earthly things." Why? Because "you died, and your life is now hidden with Christ in God" (Colossians 3:1-3).

As a result of being hidden in Christ and having our hearts and minds on things above, our bodies follow suit and put to death "whatever belongs to your earthly nature: sexual immorality, impurity, lust, evil desires and greed, which is idolatry." We rid our lives of "anger, rage, malice, slander, and filthy language from your lips" (verses 5-8). Instead, we behave as Christ Himself behaves, and put on the new man, as it were. We practice "compassion, kindness, humility, gentleness and patience." We are not quick to judge and censure, but "bear with each other and forgive whatever grievances you may have against one another" (verses 12-14).

Once saved by grace I am no longer the person I was before. People don't wallow in the mud—pigs do. So once I leave the pig farm to join human society I can no longer enjoy the mud baths that felt so good in the past. I am now adopted into God's family, and belong in the company of kings and princes. No more can I act like a beggar, no more can I live like a bum. I must walk like a prince, speak like a prince, dress like a prince, and live like a prince. Being saved by grace must change me; it must change my attitude toward sin.

That's why Paul is so assertive when he speaks against grace abuse. "Shall we continue in sin, that grace may abound?" Paul demanded, then answered his own question with the explosive, "God forbid! How shall we, that are dead to sin, live any longer therein?" (Romans 6:1, 2, KJV). Making the same argument he made to the Colossians, Paul insists that a Christian saved by grace, baptized into Christ's death, and risen through His resurrection ought also like Christ to "live a new life."

"Count yourselves dead to sin but alive to God in Christ Jesus. Therefore do not let sin reign in your mortal body so that you obey its evil desires. Do not offer the parts of your body to sin, as instruments of wickedness, but rather offer yourselves to God, as those who have been brought from death to life; and offer the parts of your body to him as instruments of righteousness" (Romans 6:11–13).

Second, saving grace places you within the boundaries of a relationship.

At 27 years of age, Joseph was energetic, muscular, and boy did he look good. Soon he caught the attention of his boss' wife, who began to feel more and more vulnerable around him.

Hesitant at first, Mrs. Potiphar finally worked up the courage to make a move on Joseph, drop him some clues by way of a smile, an admiring glance, a little flirtation. When Joseph showed no interest, she intensified her tactics. As the days turned to weeks and weeks to months, and the lustful woman's passions climbed to heights that she could now barely control, she became more and more aggressive, and eventually told Joseph quite matter-of-factly what she wanted from him: *make love to me!* (Genesis 39:7).

When Joseph still refused and Potiphar's wife realized nothing she did would convince him to sleep with her, she grabbed him by his clothes and began forcing herself on him. Being "well-built," Joseph worked himself out of his clothes and fled the crime scene, leaving his garment in the shamed woman's hands (Genesis 39:7–14).

Looking at Joseph's reaction to Mrs. Potiphar's proposal in the two short verses of Genesis 39, you will notice that he refers to Potiphar either as "my master," "he," or "his" at least five times, then concludes his response focusing on the relationship that mattered most of all to him: that with his God. "'How then could I do such a wicked thing and sin against God?'" (verses 8, 9).

Notice Joseph's first thought was not whether he could keep the affair with the mistress a secret. It was not about potential rewards or bragging rights with his peers, but about his most treasured relationships: with his master and with his God.

In the face of insurmountable temptations, Joseph saw beyond himself. He saw beyond Potiphar's wife, however alluring, delightful, or aggressive she may have been in her advances. Joseph perceived his master, Potiphar, and his God, standing right beside him, looking over his shoulders. These relationships meant more to him than sexual gratification, than the prospect of honor or glory, than his very dear life.

Chuck Swindoll spoke well when he said on his radio program *Insight for Living*, "Our conception of sin is molded by our idea of God. Light, frivolous view of God; light, frivolous view of sin. Deep and abiding sense of the holiness of God is a deep, fearful sense of sin. Our idea of God determines our concept of sin."[47] That is so true.

When our relationship with God is our most prized treasure; when pleasing Him takes precedence over the desires of a spouse, the demands of a boss, the hormones raging in our bodies, or the temptations of self-pleasure, power, or quick wealth, then we will challenge ourselves at all costs to seek first His approbation, and will think twice before we abuse the grace that He has so lavishly showered upon us. Show me your attitude toward sin, and I will tell you exactly what your view of God is.

That brings us to our final reason for escaping counterfeit grace.

Third, grace does not always revoke the consequences of sin.

In his book *What's So Amazing About Grace?* Yancey alludes to a caution offered by Lewis Smedes. He writes that forgiveness is not the same as pardon. It is very possible to offer forgiveness to someone, "'slice away the wrong from the person who did it,'" to the point that he or she is completely disconnected from that hurtful act committed against you, yet "still insist on a just punishment for that wrong."[48]

There is not one sin you commit that God cannot forgive. If your prayer for forgiveness is sincere, and your pledge to abandon the sin is real, you can be sure that the Lord will immediately wipe the slate clean. "'I, even I, am he who blots out your transgressions, for my own sake, and remembers your sins no more'" God declares (Isaiah 43:25). It is with pleasure that He removes your infringements as far from you as the east stands from west (Psalm 103:12). He longs to forgive and entreats us to work things out with Him. "'Come now, let us reason together,' says the Lord. 'Though your sins are like scarlet, they shall be as white as snow; though they are red as crimson, they shall be like wool'" (Isaiah 1:18).

But make no mistake: sin has consequences! "Before you yield to the temptation to abuse the grace God extends to you, spend some time considering the consequences. The scars of such a decision could mark you for life. Sins can be forgiven, but some scars cannot be erased."[49]

David, a man after God's own heart, was forgiven every transgression against Bathsheba and Uriah. However forgiveness did not prevent his sins' consequences. "' "The sword will never depart from your house" '" God said to David by way of Nathan the prophet. "' "Out of your own household I am going to bring calamity on you. Before your very eyes I will take your wives and give them to one who is close to you, and he will sleep with your wives in broad daylight. You did it in secret, but I will do this thing in broad daylight before all Israel" '" (2 Samuel 12:10–12; see the fulfillment in 2 Samuel 16:21–23).

Was David forgiven? No doubt. "'The Lord has taken away your sin. You are not going to die'" (2 Samuel 12:13), but he paid dearly for his transgressions. The first child born from the affair died (2 Samuel 12:15–18). At least two sons rebelled against his kingdom and paid for that with their lives: Absalom (2 Samuel 15) and Adonijah (1 Kings 1, 2). David's sin led to sibling rivalry, incest, murder, and all kinds of depraved acts under his very roof.

Forgiveness did not mean everything was now hunky-dory. He paid very dearly for his transgressions.

Stick your hand into a fiery oven and you will suffer the burns. Sin leaves its own marks. God's forgiveness may come immediately, and time will eventually heal the wounds. But the scars will remain. Some decisions will require a lifetime to repair; others will leave you with irreparable damages that must be endured for the remainder of your natural life—debts that must be paid in blood, sweat, and tears.

Do not allow God's delay in dealing with sin to fool you into abusing grace. "Although a wicked man commits a hundred crimes and still lives a long time, I know that it will go better with God-fearing men, who are reverent before God" (Ecclesiastes 8:12). You can be sure of this: "Your sin will find you out!" (Numbers 32:23, KJV).

LAST WORDS
Grace Transforms

THE word metamorphosis refers to the transformation of someone or something. It can be a physical change, such as a body of water turning to ice; it can be a change in appearance or circumstances, like when a tadpole metamorphoses into a frog or a caterpillar morphs into a beautiful butterfly; it can also be a spiritual, supernatural transformation, which results when faith creates intimacy with God and grace happens to you.

After hearing Jesus' words, "'Go and sin no more,'" His grace must have shocked the prostitution out of the woman. The transition from a woman of the night to a follower of Jesus must have taken some time. There were old habits to break, new habits to form, and lessons to unlearn, but she turned her life around and thenceforth became one of Jesus' most ardently devoted servants.

Many Bible scholars have identified Mary Magdalene and Mary

of Bethany, the sister of Martha and Lazarus, as one and the same person. According to that view the woman introduced in the John 8 story is this same Mary, and John 8 is believed to have been her very first encounter with Jesus.[50] On at least seven occasions following the John 8 account, we find Mary with Jesus.

She accompanied Christ during His second Galilean tour (Luke 8:1–3), sat at His feet as He taught during what was probably His first visit to her Bethany home, which she shared with her sister Martha and brother Lazarus (Luke 10:38–42).

Mary also threw herself at Jesus' feet in her moment of intense grief, following the death and burial of her beloved brother Lazarus. "'Lord, if you had been here, my brother would not have died,'" she agonized (John 11:32).

The next encounter between Mary and Jesus is one recorded in all four Gospels. Jesus was at a feast in the home of Simon the Pharisee, thrown in His favor for healing Simon of leprosy. Grateful for the grace that Christ had sumptuously lavished on her, Mary risked the stares and censures of the Bethany public and used the extravagant feast as an occasion to uniquely express her gratitude to Jesus.

When Christ was on the cross, nailed between Barabbas's two accomplices;[51] when in the agony of His soul He bore the curse of our sins, with the vast throng crying for His blood as the crowd cried for hers; when He was abandoned by the disciples; when He felt forsaken by the Father and abandoned by His subjects in the courts of heaven; when His lifeless form was being removed from the cross and buried in a stony cave, Mary tarried near. She was among the last few to remain by His side (Matthew 27:57–61; Mark 15:42–47).

On that great resurrection morning, "at dawn on the first day of the week," Mary Magdalene was among the first disciples to rush to the empty tomb (Matthew 28:1). She was with the other women when the two angels announced Christ's resurrection (Luke 24:4–7), and was the last remaining disciple when everyone else had left the tomb. There she was, in deep trepidation mingled with bewilderment, agonizing over the apparent stolen body of the Savior. And upon this occasion, Christ showed Himself first and foremost to this former prostitute.

Christ's resurrection was the crowning achievement of His work on earth as Redeemer of the world. Without it, the whole plan of salvation would have imploded. The assurance and firmness of the gospel is solidified in it; the personal witness of the resurrection is what gave power to the apostles' preaching. The resurrection confirmed Christ as Son of God. The gospel, faith, salvation—all prove vain without Christ's resurrection from the dead, because through it He is glorified. So the honor of being the first to behold the risen Christ is no small privilege.

Yet Jesus did not first show Himself to His earthly mother. He did not first appear to His eleven remaining disciples, nor to His enemies to say "I told you so!" Before Christ even presented Himself to the Father in heaven with power and glory to ascertain that His sacrifice had been accepted;[52] before being welcomed by powerful angels who would blast resplendent golden trumpets, thrust glistening crowns at His feet and prostrate themselves in praise before Him, Christ tarried on earth long enough to be seen first by an unworthy sinner with a shameful past and a butchered reputation.

The grace that redeemed Mary from a life of shame and self-destructive behaviors is the same grace that God extends to you and me today. Right where you are, amid your misdeeds, His arms are lovingly extended toward you as His heart pleads with yours, "Come to Me!"

The funny thing about grace is that those who think they can't afford it are the ones better postured to receive it, and those who think they need none of it are in direst privation for it. No matter who you are, or what your situation is, God has enough love to engulf your need for acceptance, enough compassion to comfort your suffering, enough patience to deal with your inconsistencies, and enough grace to cover your multitude of transgressions.

So come!

Weary and heavy laden, "Come!"

Sin has wrecked the very structure of your life, "Come!"

Shame causes you to retreat into a cave, afraid of what others will think of the mess you have made of your life, "Come!"

You are suffering the repercussions of bad decisions and past mistakes, "Come!"

It matters little where you are, what you have done, how deeply you have sunk into the miry pit of wickedness. Today grace is extended to you, on the house, just as it was to this woman caught in the process of prostituting herself. Your case is not hopeless; it is not too late. Jesus still cares. He is yet again compassionate and gracious, slow to anger and abounding in love. So come to Him. He still loves, still cares, still delivers.

Grace can happen to you!

CULMINATION

Faith Gives Audacity

7

GIANTS OF OUR LIVES

GIANTS ARE NOT necessarily creatures that exist only in fairy tale legends. They are not only mythological beings that are taller, stronger, and larger than the average person. Giants come in all shapes and sizes, and every one of us confronts them.

We face giants in the bedroom with a contentious wife or an unloving, brutish husband; at the office with a demanding, unreasonable boss. Sometimes the giants are friends, sometimes neighbors, other times enemies. They come in the form of tough economic challenges, crippling diseases, nightmarish natural calamities, or sins that easily beset us. Our giant can be visible, a disfiguration that stares us down when we look in the mirror; or it can be invisible, a tumor lodged somewhere in the brain.

It is a fact of life: giants are inevitable, but they are not invincible. Men of faith have gained insights into the secret to giant slaying. From Joseph's faceoff with Potiphar's licentious wife to Moses' showdown with the stubborn-as-a-mule Pharaoh of Egypt; from David's famous bout with the nearly-ten-foot-tall Goliath to each and every one of us who today face more sophisticated, technologically advanced, 21st century giants, God has given us the ability to stand up to, fight, and defeat our giants.

FAITH GIVES AUDACITY

THE word audacity has a hint of rebelliousness, an air of defiance. A person of audacity is not one to simply submit to the order of things. He abhors regularity, has a blatant disregard for normalcy, and often ventures where others would never dare. Not that he is a rule breaker, but the man with audacity is not quick to conform to the box that societal norms often try to confine him to. He is bold, unflinching, stares fear down until it whimpers and retreats to its corner. He is the kind of man you would call gutsy, resolute, dauntless.

When you have matured in faith and become intimate with God, the relationship culminates in an audacity that is more than mere valor.

Audacity takes our faith to the grandest scale of our relationship with God. This kind of faith is outrageous. When it is boiling in your veins you cannot be content to play the victim or walk around chanting "Woe is me!" because life knocks you down a bit. When the going gets rough, audacity provides the drive to grab life by the throat. It puts your faith in overdrive and gives you the gumption to face your pain with courage. Trouble may abound, and when it does, your faith super-abounds! A man with the audacity that faith gives is never content with second best.

That does not make all heroes of faith successful by the world's standards. Their definition of success is not wealth and fame; it is not the size of their wallet, but the reach of their faith; not by how much influence they exert on others but by how closely knit their hearts are with God's heart.

The audacity of faith does not make you invincible, like some unrealistic James Bond type. A man of faith still suffers loss. He faces abysmal circumstances with the same initial reaction of shock and disbelief as the average person. He still reels from pain. And yes, that fearless man of faith may still die in the fight.

But when the world tends to look around, the man of faith looks up. When others look within for a way out of their predicaments, he looks to God. The source of his pluckiness is not himself, his intellect, connections, bank accounts, or gadgets. His intrepidity does not stem from his own prowess and perspicacity. The power that lights his bulb finds its source worlds away from planet earth. He does not stake his claims on his feeble muscles, but upon the overwhelming strength of the arms that hold the universe in place.

Men with the audacity of faith are also not afraid to be peculiar. They understand that Jesus was the most peculiar Man to ever live. He was not part of the "in" crowd, was not a Man of conventional wisdom and ways. The man with the audacity of faith models his life after the life of Christ, and as such, will most likely come across a little weird.

This faith is not what most skeptics tend to see as unintelligent acquiescence. It is, rather, a deeply rooted, solidly founded, fire-proof trust in a God who is all-powerful and all knowing. This nonpareil reliance on God's ability and integrity is gained through life scars and grueling experiences. Having been around the block with God, and learned to totally trust His ways, is what frees His hands to do incredible things for us. It is what emboldens our hearts, stiffens our spines, outstretches our reaches, enlarges our visions, defeats our fears, and aligns our hearts with His.

A Friend in High Places

Have you ever wondered why some of our biblical heroes were so bold? They made iron float, walked on water, raised the dead, and split a sea in two. Even Hollywood has a hard time replicating some of these miracles—and they use computer animation. These men never flinched before great enemies in their pomp or nature in its swelling pride. They had a boldness that makes us shiver. Consider this young man's face-off with the greatest emperor the world had ever known.

There he was, only about nineteen or twenty years old. He woke up one day to a crisis: the emperor had said, "Off with the heads of all of the land's intellectuals!" Why? Because they were all incompetent. They could not solve what seemed, to his highness, a simple problem. He'd had a dream the night before, and wanted his wise men to interpret its meaning. By the way, the king had also forgotten what the dream was about. The wise men's job, as Nebuchadnezzar saw it, was to tell him the details of his dream and give him an explanation for it.

Simple enough, right? I don't think so either.

The wise men—the professors, researchers, royal advisors, scientists, magicians, astrologers, sorcerers, priests—were scrambling to find something favorable to tell the king, something to calm his nerves. It was either that or procrastinate long enough for the matter to lose its urgency. But Nebuchadnezzar was on to them. He wanted an answer, and he wanted it before breakfast!

The men protested. What the king was asking for was impossible, unreasonable—something no king, no matter how great, had ever demanded of anyone who wore their sandals. Nebuchadnezzar did not care. "'If you do not tell me what my dream was and interpret it,'" he warned, "'I will have you cut into pieces and your houses turned into piles of rubble!'" (Daniel 2:5).

When it became clear that he wouldn't be given an answer, Nebuchadnezzar called Arioch, the captain of his bodyguards, and told him to kill everyone in the Wise Man branch of the government. Anyone with a job title of "advisor," "magician," "diviner," or anything along those lines, was suddenly in danger of losing his head.

This is where things got sticky for Daniel.

He was fresh out of a three-year reeducation program under the tutelage of Babylon's most illustrious teachers. During that period Daniel was taught science, language, literature, mathematics, management, accounting, engineering, finance, sorcery—all subjects that he aced when tested by the king himself. Upon graduation he became part of the royal entourage, a member of the Wise Man department, which meant his head, too, was wanted by Nebuchadnezzar. But look at Daniel's reaction to the king's edict.

Instead of making a run for it or sinking into a depression like the rest of the wise men, Daniel went to the emperor and asked for *time*. Twenty-four hours was all he needed. He would phone a Friend, Someone in the business of solving impossible puzzles and who had the wherewithal to overwhelm any situation. He promised the emperor that by the same time the next day, he would have not only the details of the dream but also its explanation.

Everyone who faced the king was fearful; everyone scrambled to find something to tell him that was either deceitful or flattering. I imagine some men begged for their lives, others tried to reason with him. Some attempted to skip town. Daniel faced the man, looked him straight in the eyes and said, "Give me twenty-four hours, your highness, and I'll have what you want!" Faith gave him the valiance to stand before the king when everyone else ran in fear.

Everyone listened to Nebuchadnezzar's requests, looked themselves in the mirror, checked their level of resources, and ran. Daniel listened to the same requests, lifted his eyes to the hills where his help came from—from the Lord, Maker of heaven and earth, who gives men the ability to dream, and knows the details of every man's thoughts—and saw no reason to fear. He knew that God's resources had so overwhelmed the king's requests that they no longer mattered. Instead of running he stared down the great monarch, and promised him that what he asked for was in fact as easy as breathing to God.

Your pilgrimage through life will pit you against some impossible odds. You may face giants with the power to obliterate you. You may stand before folks who, with simple words, can take away your livelihood, ruin your career, destroy your self-confidence, and maybe even take your life. How you respond will be in direct proportion to the audacity of your faith.

When at life's dangerous crossroads, when the options are only bad and worse, do not look within. Never think of yourself, your training, wealth, influence, or earthly connections. Instead look up! Check your connection with the Almighty, ensure His line is open to you. Make a call to Him, and let Him put His resources at your disposal. At that point you will see your problems in a brand new light. They may not disappear, but knowing they are now God's problems will give you peace of mind to bear their weight until God eventually solves them.

WHAT'S FAITH GOT TO DO WITH IT?

"IF you ride the biggest roller coaster in the world, the kid's ride at the country fair won't scare you. If you live through a hurricane and a tornado, a spring rain won't intimidate you. And when you truly know the God of the universe, people's opinions will no longer hold you hostage. Everything that once controlled you quickly loses all its power."[53]

Imagine being a Navy SEAL and showing up to a fight armed to the teeth. You have your rocket launcher hung on one shoulder, grenades at your sides, and your M249 machine gun and high-powered semiautomatic rifles are at your disposal. You are clad in protective gears as you move stealthily, seeking out the enemy. To your surprise, the enemy turns out to be an untrained, rosy-cheeked little boy with a slingshot. "Is this some kind of a joke?" you marvel in disbelief. But it is no joke. The fight is indeed against a twelve-year old adversary and his toy. You would most likely think the fight unfair, and would see absolutely no reason at all to fear.

It is impossible to be intimate with the great God of the universe, the King of kings and Lord of Lords, and still be crippled by fear. God is far too great for that. The devil may be cunning; your enemies may be impressive, but they are nothing compared with the might and depth and breadth of the God you serve. He has enough power and resources to neutralize whatever your particular threat might be.

As people of faith, all of heaven's resources are at our disposal. We've got the rocket launcher, the tank, the high-powered semiautomatic rifle, the Blackhawk, the fighter jets *and* the nuclear arsenals locked and loaded, ready for action. God's unstoppable, unassailable army, composed of myriads of powerful spiritual beings, stand ready to back us up when threatened by enemy forces. So why are we often so afraid?

Threats should not shake our confidence when it is in God. Tough talk does not sway us when we know we have His guaranteed protection. Life circumstances are measured, controlled, and directed by the very hands of God; His Word holds the universe together. So there is no need to fear the empty words or tough talk of fleeting, feeble men who forget that they are nothing more than blocks of animated dirt.

This does not mean God will simply write us a blank check, give whatever we ask or come at the moment we expect. Having enough faith to trust that He will, however, is what makes men like Moses and Daniel and David and Samuel and Elisha so reckless in their faith. It is what led Elijah to order the rain to stop for three-and-a-half years and it did. It is what can lead you and me to face today's circumstances with confidence and boldness.

Søren Kierkegaard calls the man with this kind of audacity a "knight of faith."

"This figure is the man who lives in faith, who has given over the meaning of his life to his Creator, and who lives centered on the energies of his Creator. He accepts whatever happens in this visible dimension without complaint, lives his life as a duty, faces his death without a qualm. No pettiness is so petty that it threatens his meanings; no task is too frightening to be beyond his courage. He is fully in the world on its terms and wholly beyond the world in his trust in the invisible dimension."[54]

GIANTS OF OUR LIVES

IN the 2001 NBA finals, the Los Angeles Lakers faced the Philadelphia 76ers in a matchup that was purely a big-guy-versus-little-guy standoff.

The Lakers were the defending champions, and they were at the top of their game. This was the time when Shaquille O'Neal was the most dominant player in the NBA and young Kobe Bryant was unstoppable. With those two at the helm of the Lakers, the team swept all three opponents faced in the playoffs to win the Western Conference finals with a flawless 12–0 record!*

The 76ers in the East, led by Allen Iverson and Dikembe Mutombo, struggled their way to the finals with a 4–3 victory over the Milwaukee Bucks (compared to LA's crushing 4–0 victory over the gigantic San Antonio Spurs). Nobody thought the 76ers stood a chance. They were the underdogs, the little guys that the Lakers would simply squash like a bug. But in the very first game of the

---

* In those days the first round of the NBA playoffs was best of five as opposed to best of seven.

series, the 76ers stopped LA dead in their tracks. They defeated the big guys, crushed their pride, and sent a message to basketball fans all over the world that giants can in fact be slain. If the NBA finals had been a one-game, do-or-die, winner-takes-all matchup, the 76ers would have won the championship.

Giants have a way of intimidating us. Imposing, threatening, overbearing, downright ugly, they flaunt their stuff in our faces to impress and terrify. Judging them on the basis of surface appearance, we are tempted to raise the white flag and surrender in defeat. But no matter how powerful and impressive your giant appears, God is greater still, and is more than capable of handling your giant.

There is a giant slayer in the Bible who, in my view, has not received enough airtime. His story, at least the beginning of it, is tucked away in an obscure book that most people shy away from. He does not get the kind of headlines that Joseph received for slaying the giant of licentiousness by staying sexually pure in Egypt; he has not gotten the kind of press Samson, the morally weak strongman of the Bible, received for his slaying of a lion and partial deliverance of Israel from the Philistines.

Nevertheless this giant-slayer received incredible props from God. His name is almost always associated with this next sentence, a testament to his exceptional strength of mind and heart: he served God wholeheartedly.

The Man Who Would Take on Giants

We first meet Caleb in the thick of the book of Numbers, about a third of the way through. After twelve chapters of census, genealogies, family legacies, sins, consequences, and religious rites, Moses pauses to tell us about the exploration of the land of Canaan before its conquest. When the people reached Kadesh-barnea, he sent twelve spies to go scout the land, giving them this command:

"'Go up through the Negev and on into the hill country. See

what the land is like and whether the people who live there are strong or weak, few or many. What kind of land do they live in? Is it good or bad? What kind of towns do they live in? Are they unwalled or fortified? How is the soil? Is it fertile or poor? Are there trees on it or not? Do your best to bring back some of the fruit of the land'" (Numbers 13:17–20).

This is our first encounter with the great Caleb, who is introduced in verse 6: "From the tribe of Judah Caleb, the son of Jephunneh."

Jephunneh was a Kenizzite (see Joshua 14:6). According to author Roy Adams, the Kenizzites were descendants of Kenaz, who was the son of Eliphaz, firstborn of Esau.[55] They were an Edomite tribal group from the very land to which Moses was sending Caleb, Joshua, and the other agents to spy. If you review the original promise made to Abraham in Genesis, you will notice that God mentioned the Kenizzites among the people whose land He would give to Abraham's descendants (Genesis 15:18, 19).

Despite his mixed heritage, Caleb was a wholehearted follower of the God of Israel, and followed Jewish customs faithfully.

Coming back from their espionage of Canaan after a period of forty days, the twelve spies, one from each tribe, returned to an awaiting throng that was full of high hopes and eager expectancy, anxious to hear the report of what the land was like. The spies brought specimens of fruits from Canaan, as commanded by Moses—giant pomegranates, figs, and a cluster of grapes so huge that two men had to carry it between them on a pole—to show the people how great and promising the soil was. You can imagine the excitement, the rapturous, joyful celebration that resulted from seeing those fruits. However the celebration was short-lived. Things quickly turned ugly when the spies began describing what they saw.

"'We went into the land to which you sent us, and it does flow with milk and honey! Here is its fruit'" (Numbers 13:27). That's the only positive report the ten spies had—two sentences, twenty-two English words from the 1984 NIV. The rest of their discourse—five verses, 108 words—was dedicated to proving to the people why they should *not* go forth and take the land. It was a message of fear and discouragement, one colored by the conditions of their hearts.

"'We can't attack those people; they are stronger than we are!'" In other words they were saying, *God's promise that He would give us that land is an illusion. We can't conquer Canaan.* "'The land we explored devours those living in it. All the people we saw there are of great size. We saw the Nephilim there (the descendants of Anak come from the Nephilim). We seemed like grasshoppers in our own eyes, and we looked the same to them'" (verses 31-33).

Their description of the land was obviously a tremendous exaggeration. How could an exceedingly good land, one that flows with milk and honey, that produces these giant fruits and men of such great stature and intellect, actually devour its people? Their tactic was intended to scare the life out of Israel, and it worked.

The spies' words sent shockwaves throughout the camp. Hope gave way to despair; rejoicing turned to bitter lament. God and His mighty acts were quickly forgotten. The destruction of Egypt's firstborn; the parting of the Red Sea; manna in the desert; water from a rock—all of these great exhibits of God's power were ancient history. It got so bad that Israel orchestrated a coup. They would remove Moses from office and elect a new leader, one who would submit to their pressure and lead them back to Egypt, back to slavery and death.

Caleb could not believe it. Watching Moses and Aaron, old men in their eighties, prostrate on the desert floor pleading with Israel, Caleb and his friend Joshua tore their clothes as a sign of sorrow

THE **AUDACITY** OF FAITH

at the people's disbelief, and made one last ditch effort to get the people on board.

"'The land we passed through and explored is exceedingly good. If the Lord is pleased with us, he will lead us into that land, a land flowing with milk and honey, and will give it to us. Only do not rebel against the Lord. *And do not be afraid of the people of the land, because we will swallow them up. Their protection is gone, but the Lord is with us.* Do not be afraid of them'" (Numbers 14:6-9).

They were saying, "Are you kiddin' me? Those people don't stand a chance! We've got God's protection! True, their walls are fortified...wasn't Egypt's army? Yeah, they're giants...wasn't Pharaoh considered a god? Their defenses aren't fortified against God. He has the muscles and brainpower to break through them. We can take 'em the way we took Egypt without drawing a sword. We can defeat them the way we did the Amalekites. Only don't question God's power and motive."

The Measure of Greatness

F. B. Meyer says about Caleb:

> Amid the marchings and counter-marchings, the innumerable deaths, the murmurings and rebellions of the people, he retained a steadfast purpose to do God's will, to please him, and to know no other leader, and to heed no other voice. It was of no use to try and involve that stout lion's cub in any movement against Moses or Aaron. He would not party to Miriam's jealous spite. He would not be allured by the wiles of the girls of Moab. Always strong and true and pure and noble; like a rock in a changeful sea, like a snowcapped peak in a change of cloud and storm and sun. A man in whose strong nature weaker men could hide, and who must have been a tower of strength to that new and young generation which grew

up to fill the vacant places in the van of Israel. The Nester of the Hebrew camp, in him the words of the Psalmist were anticipated, that he bore fruit in his old age, and to the last was fat and flourishing.[56]

What a man!

Caleb breathed air, bled red, and sweated salty fluids like the rest of us. The secret to this former slave's incredible boldness was an utter surrender and unreserved trust in God. He kept his faith glasses on when the powerful giants of Canaan appeared too overwhelming to conquer, and the lens of faith reduced them to midgets. The secret of his success, James Montgomery Boice writes, is that "he had his eyes on God and not on the vacillating and terrifying things around him."

Throughout Numbers 13 and 14, as people describe Canaan, no matter who is speaking the descriptions remain consistent. 1) The land is an exceedingly good land. 2) It flows with milk and honey. 3) The cities are fortified. 4) The people are numerous and they are giants. Caleb depicted the land this way, as did Joshua, as did the ten other spies. The difference, as Boice observes, is not in *what* they saw, but in *Who* they compared what they saw to.

"The ten [spies] looked at themselves and the giants and concluded that a conquest of those people was impossible. Compared to the giants, the Jews seemed like grasshoppers. Caleb and Joshua looked at God rather than circumstances, and when compared to God, the giants were grasshoppers."[57]

When you pit your problems against yourself, when you compare the bills to your account balance, the disease to your health insurance coverage or your doctor's knowledge or reputation, when you compare the mount you have to climb to the strength of your bootstraps, then you will despair when the odds stock high against you. You will retreat into a corner when circumstances prove foreboding, when trials prove too overwhelming.

But when you put on your pair of faith lenses, the God of omnipotence and omniscience becomes the One against Whom your problems are pitted. Although your giants remain great in size, although you do not grow a few feet taller or put on a few extra pounds of muscle weight, your giants appear to shrink in size when you see them from God's perspective. You then have the audacity to stand your ground because God Himself stands with you.

True greatness is the ability to live in the shadow of God's wings and view life from His perspective. You cannot lose, cannot falter when God is your energy source.

The audacity that comes from faith does not take us away from reality. Instead it reveals the greater reality that God is sovereignly in charge, that He is greater than any giant you could ever face in life. Terrible life circumstances don't scare Him, and when He stands next to you, they should not scare you either. Insurmountable ordeals do not impress Him, nor should they impress you. Before the awesomeness of the "'God of gods and Lord of lords, the great God, mighty and awesome'" (Deuteronomy 10:17) all of our giants, no matter how impressive, become midgets.

The Faith that Keeps You Going

Having learned of the Canaanites' fortified cities and people of great stature, "All the Israelites grumbled against Moses and Aaron, and the whole assembly said to them, 'If only we had died in Egypt! Or in this desert!'" (Numbers 14:2). We are not talking about a couple hundred people coming to Moses to calmly complain about things they didn't like. This was a rebellious throng estimated at about two million, beset by anger and frustration, bereft of reason, and loud in their denunciations of Moses and Aaron and Caleb and Joshua. It was a chaotic scene where the mob went insane, grabbing huge stones to murder Caleb and Joshua for daring to defend God. It was so bad that God Himself had to intervene. His glory, like a flaming light, illuminated the tabernacle, and the crowd quieted down. God then proceed to give them *exactly* what they asked for.

God said, "'As surely as I live and as surely as the glory of the Lord fills the whole earth, not one of the men who saw my glory and the miraculous signs I performed in Egypt and in the desert but who disobeyed me and tested me 10 times—not one of them will ever see the land I promised on oath to their forefathers. No one who has treated me with contempt will ever see it'" (Numbers 14:21-23).

"'Your bodies will fall in this desert. Your children will be shepherds here for forty years, suffering for your unfaithfulness, until the last of your bodies lies in the desert. For forty years—one year for each of the forty days you explored the land—you will suffer for your sins and know what it is like to have me against you'" (verse 32-34).

While He passed judgment against Israel, God singled out Caleb for his faithfulness. "'Because my servant Caleb has a different spirit and *follows me wholeheartedly,* I will bring him into the land he went to, and his descendants will inherit it'" (verse 24).

The word "wholeheartedly" appears in many other passages where Caleb's name is mentioned (Numbers 32:12; Joshua 14:8; Deuteronomy 1:36). It refers to a man who gave himself to God sincerely, unreservedly, completely. His was not a halfhearted, grudgingly compliant service. Caleb did not serve God part-time, sometimes, or when there was time. He was not a tepid believer, the type who loves God when the bills are paid or when disaster strikes. He was an all-around, day-in day-out man of faith who put it all on the line for God. He had "a different spirit" within him; the honor of God was of greater value than riches, of greater value than the favor and accolades of men, of greater value than life. That was what kept Caleb strong.

Caleb was not launched into Canaan ahead of disobedient Israel. He remained in the wilderness forty years while the rest of the people—every man twenty years and older—faded into oblivion. Can you imagine serving a life sentence for somebody else's crime?

Still Caleb did not give in to bitterness. Disappointed? Yes. Sorely frustrated? Absolutely. Nevertheless he accepted the divine mandate, and waited for God's sentence to be fully served. His faith never wavered. Tested and tried, suffering though innocent, this faithful giant slayer came forth as gold.

Those forty years brought plagues, diseases, the perils of warfare, and other untold dangers. Caleb remained strong. Like a vessel tossed by the angry oceans, like a reed whipped about in the storm, he bore the punishment of the wicked and faithless while clinging to his God. And after an entire generation passed from the scene, this old man was left standing because he served the Lord wholeheartedly.

Faith keeps us going. When others run out of steam and feel the need to take a pause, faith cries "Forward!" When the vicissitudes of daily life cause fear, worry, anxiety, and saps our strength, faith gives us the fortitude to stand firm. It keeps us strong when the passage of time abuses our bodies, when diseases eat away at our vitality, when pressed against the ropes, on the verge of defeat, powerless, hopeless, and when every sight that meets our eyes yells, "Give up!"

Faith says, "Hold on, don't let go," even when disappointment comes, when discouragement sets in. Rather than focusing on the fluctuating circumstances of our surroundings, faith keeps our focus on God. It gives us, in Chuck's Swindoll's words, a vertical perspective.

Nothing is easier, especially in the middle of a storm, than keeping our focus on the blowing winds, falling trees, and flying debris. It takes no great effort to keep a horizontal perspective—to focus on ourselves or on others, to mope along, throw ourselves a pity party. But a horizontal perspective weakens us. It causes us to respond to the flesh, makes us want to get even, to treat people as they treat us. It gives us a shortsighted view of life.

A vertical perspective strengthens us. It reminds us that God is sovereign, that He is ultimately in control, and that nothing in life takes Him by surprise. It girds our loins to face life's challenges, gives us the confidence to stay the course no matter what life throws our way. It reminds us that God is heretofore on His throne, and as long as He is up there, we have no reason to fear.

Time to Collect

At age eighty-five, after thirty-eight years of waiting and seven years of fighting for the conquest of Canaan, Caleb was just getting started. He had a full agenda of giant slaying left to do, and was not about to retire before doing it. Listen to his daring declaration to Joshua, the other faithful spy and Israel's intrepid leader after Moses' death:

> I was forty years old when Moses the servant of the Lord sent me from Kadesh Barnea to explore the land. And I brought him back a report according to my convictions.... So on that day Moses swore to me, "The land on which your feet have walked will be your inheritance and that of your children forever, because you have followed the Lord my God wholeheartedly...." Here I am today, eighty-five years old! *I am still as strong today as the day Moses sent me out; I'm just as vigorous to go out to battle now as I was then.* Now give me this hill country that the Lord promised me that day. You yourself heard then that the Anakites were there and their cities were large and

fortified, *but, the Lord helping me, I will drive them out
just as he said!* (Joshua 14:8-12).

I love it!

These are bold words for a senior citizen. Eighty-five was a good
age to hang up the gloves, set aside the cleats, retire the old jersey.
As Boice observes, Caleb was a good twenty years past retirement
age. About half the men his age would have been bound to a wheelchair or hospital bed by now. Those fortunate enough to be moving
around would most likely have been in no condition to take up
arms and go off to war.

Yet this great man declared himself as strong at eighty-five as
he had been at forty, as prepared to take on the giants of Hebron
at this stage as he was back then. His faith had not been abated;
his dedication to God and His cause remained intact. His loyalty,
drive, and passion for righteousness were as strong now as then.
And as a result God preserved his physical strength.

It was not because Caleb had anything to prove—he didn't. The
veteran warrior had paid his dues and then some. He had been
Moses' strong supporter, and after Moses' death, he remained an
even stronger force for Joshua. The last seven years of his life had
been spent on the battlefield with the rest of the army fighting for
the conquest of Canaan. One could argue that Caleb had earned
the right for a good inheritance and was well deserving of a break;
that he qualified for a nice plot of already-conquered land where he
could relax and watch the grandkids play in the fields.

Instead the man chose Hebron as his inheritance—uncon-
quered, giant-infested Hebron, the place that had struck terror in
the hearts of the other ten spies forty-five years prior. In the end
Caleb led a successful campaign against Hebron, driving out its
giants (Joshua 15:14).

Notice that, in spite of Caleb's vigor and strength, he did not rely on himself to win on the battlefield or in life. It was not bravery, natural abilities, mental acuity or an uncanny ability to get into his enemy's head that led to Caleb's successful life of giant slaying. Most or all of these may have been true about the man, but the very reason why Caleb succeeded where the other ten spies, a whole generation of Israelites, and most of us today fail, is the single factor of faith—the kind of faith that offers heart service. He lived his life to the pleasure and satisfaction of no one and nothing other than God Himself. Caleb lived his life to the pleasure of "the Audience of One."

LAST WORDS
Faith Seeks the Last, Highest Audience

IN his masterful book *The Call* Os Guinness has a chapter entitled "The Audience of One." It is an invitation to live life before the only eyes that matter, speak from our hearts to the only ears that truly make the difference and are ever attentive, and to live purposefully "above and beyond the impossible-to-satisfy constituencies." It invites us to live our lives, order our steps, and direct our thoughts and deeds to the one audience that trumps all others, that last, highest audience—the Audience of One!

Most of us, Guinness writes, live life with an eye to the approval of some audience. Some people perform for a spouse. Some direct their performance to the attention of a boss, a neighbor, a brother, or a friend. Some, like certain celebrities, target the general public. Even some of our religious friends tailor their performances to the attention of "lesser audiences." Ultimately, each one of us lives for the pleasure of some viewer, seen or unseen. But the one who through faith reaches Caleb's level of intimacy with God will strive to live for that one great Audience, the Audience of One.

Your life takes on a whole new dimension when you live for the Audience of One. You don't live for the opinions of men, nor are your actions tailored to please the senses of those who take gallop polls or instigate hallway gossips. Their love or hate does not govern who you are or what you do. Instead of putting on a façade, of racing to center stage so onlookers can see how great you are and give you accolades for a job well done, you try instead to live for the eye that can see what is happening inside of you, the One more concerned with your heart's message than your lips', who reads your thoughts and knows your motives.

Living before that Audience is utterly difficult. Awareness of Him is not always at the forefront of our consciousness, mainly because He does not readily point out our frailties or air our dirty laundries for all to see, as the swarm of other audiences tends to do. As a result we often forget that He matters, live instead for the pleasures of inconsequential audiences whose barks are loudest but whose bites matter little in the grand scheme of things.

Should we live for the Audience of One, whose opinions alone will matter when the great hand of time strikes the hour when all deeds must be confronted, we would be impervious to the applauses, smiles, criticisms, or scathes of those around us. We would watch our thoughts and words, actions and reactions, not to be acknowledged by our peers, who are as lost and broken as we are, but to please the heart of Him who made us and who alone can save us. If He smiles on us, then the smiles or frowns of men matter little.

Faith Leaves a Mark

8

GOD PLACED A BET

"THERE ARE TRIUMPHANT defeats that rival victories," French philosopher Montaigne once said. This proves true for professional golfer Brian Davis.

Davis was trying to win his first PGA Tour against former U.S. Open and multiple PGA Tour winner Jim Furyk. His approach shot on the first hole of the playoff bounced off the green, and the ball landed in a hazard that had clusters of reeds. According to the rules, a player or his club cannot hit any impediment during a shot; that constitutes a violation. A practice swing seemed to have cleared the reeds, but when Davis hit the actual shot, from the corner of his eyes he thought that he might have touched one of the reeds.

Davis immediately called a penalty on himself, prompting the rules official to order a review of the TV monitors. It was a minor violation, indiscernible except through slow motion replays. Nevertheless it came with a two-stroke penalty, which essentially meant game over for Davis, and he knew it. Once the violation was confirmed, Davis conceded the victory to Jim Furyk, who clinched his fifteenth career win and a grand prize of $1,026,000. Davis, for

155

his part, went home a loser that day, failing to quality for major championships and other exemptions.

It is a rarity in our day to find men of character, men who refuse to be bought or sold, men who will stand for the right when no one is looking, when it is easy to benefit from a wrong act and get away with it, men of deep conviction, who would rather suffer loss than to auction away their dignity, men who live their lives not for self, not for gains, not for the pleasures of the watching public, but for the eyes and pleasure of the Audience of One.

Davis lost the championship game that day, but this defeat was one of his greatest victories. I had never heard of Brian Davis before, and probably never would have had it not been for his courageous act of character. As one sportswriter put it, he was not "the best-known name in golf—or even the hundredth best known." But his action was worthy of media coverage, and he used the attention to promote the Skin Cancer Foundation, for which he volunteered as a spokesperson.

Sometimes it pays to lose! No, it will not feel good. It will not always get you praise from peers and from the media; it will not always leave you standing to tell about it the next day. But certain shellackings are worth the bother. If you are a man or woman of faith, you can be sure that, at one point or another during your faith pilgrimage, you will suffer apparent defeat.

We all love a faith story with happy ending. We love it when Joseph, after all of his sufferings, ends up becoming prime minister of Egypt. We are thrilled that Shadrach, Meshach, and Abednego, honorable men of faith and of spotless character, escaped the fiery furnace. We long to hear more stories like that of Daniel, who not only rose to prominence in two different pagan empires—Babylon and Medo-Persia—but by God's grace defeated all of his enemies and walked away unscathed from the den of hungry lions.

But read the Bible long enough and we discover that there are "others" of the faith who died in the fight. There are others, like the apostle Peter, who ended up crucified upside down. There are others, like the apostle Paul, who ended up beheaded. Some, like the prophet Isaiah, were sawed in half.

Nevertheless know this: no matter the apparent defeat, faith never loses. When you surrender your life to God in pursuit of holiness; when you serve Him faithfully, fight the good fight, run the race, even when it seems you have lost, you are yet, and forever, the victor!

FAITH LEAVES A MARK

I once heard the dramatic story of the choice that a Haitian boy had to make to survive the devastating earthquake that struck Haiti on January 12, 2010.

Following the 31-second earthquake, the boy found himself buried beneath the rubble of a collapsed building, with one of his legs pinned down under heavy concrete. Unable to move or free himself, the child simply lay there, waiting to die. When rescuers found him he learned that his only chance of survival was to sever his leg, but that was not the worst news.

Because of where he was located and the obstacles surrounding him, rescuers instructed him that they could not perform the amputation—he would have to do it himself, without anesthesia. Courageously the young child, after a few instructions from rescue workers, took the saw from them and sawed off his own leg.

That fateful day will remain forever etched in this child's memory. He will relive it every time he puts on a shoe, every time he tries to walk to the bathroom, every time he moves the damaged limb. No matter where he goes, or what he becomes, he will always carry with him the mark of that great devastation—physically and emotionally. It will be a perpetual reminder of the day his life was forever transformed.

Like the missing limb of that young Haitian boy, faith leaves an indelible mark on the lives of its possessors. The faith that brings intimacy with God imprints the character of Christ upon us. You can tell people of faith from a mile away. It's nearly impossible for them to conceal who they are, to not appear peculiar to the world at large. Ask the apostle Peter.

Peter tried very hard to conceal his identify that fateful night when they arrested Jesus. He hid in the shadows, claimed he had never met the Man now being scourged, even spewed out a few expletives to prove he never knew Jesus. But his speech betrayed him. Something about the presence of Christ in one's life, about His ability to change hearts and minds, always leaves folks who've been exposed to Him with a mark. They tend to walk like Him, to sound like Him. They tend to have a hard time fitting into society, succumbing to societal norms, because Christ had such a hard time fitting in. If you've run into Christ at some point in your life and have allowed Him to make a new creature out of you (see 1 Corinthians 5:17), then for the rest of your days, you will bear the mark of His character (see Acts 4:13).

Jacob never forgot the night He met Christ.

The aged patriarch was not having a good year. In fact, the past twenty years had been rather rough. Jacob deceived his father, stole his brother's blessings, and then ran away from home when his brother Esau set out to whack him. He moved in with his uncle Laban, proposed marriage to one of his cousins—the gorgeous younger sister with the model-like figure and the pretty face—only to wake up the day after the wedding in bed with the older sister, the not-so-pretty one with the funny eyes. He ended up marrying the younger sister as well, then hooked up with the sisters' maids, eventually getting twelve sons and a daughter from the four women warring for his affection.

His abusive uncle and cousins rose up against Jacob, accusing him of theft and manipulation, prompting Jacob to stealthily gather his family, pack up his belongings, and run back home. A heavy burden weighed on his heart, because he knew his older brother Esau had not forgotten the events of twenty years prior, when Jacob stole his blessings. Instead of throwing Jacob a welcome home party, Esau was now approaching him with a band 400-strong.

In trepidation, Jacob turned to prayer. With his family separated into two groups, he spent the night alone at God's feet, admitting his unworthiness and begging for divine intervention. There, on the darkest night of his life, Jacob came face to face with the Savior Himself. As he prayed, Christ came down from heaven to meet him, to assure him of God's protection. The Lord placed a hand upon Jacob's shoulder, to console, comfort, and strengthen him.

But Jacob was in a mountainous region, a dangerous place full of wild beasts, robbers, and murderers. Thinking it was some scoundrel who had come to take his life or possessions, he grabbed the assailant and began a wrestling match. For the next six hours Jacob would wrestle with Christ. But what mortal man can truly wrestle with the Lord of heaven? He handily defeated the devil and threw him out of heaven. So as dawn neared, Christ simply touched the socket of Jacob's hip and dislocated it. Yet Jacob would not let up. Realizing by now with Whom he was wrestling, Jacob decided to simply hold on until he received a blessing.

Jacob lost the wrestling match that dark night, of that we are certain. But it was a most triumphant defeat, because he won by losing. He won a new character, a new identify. He was no longer Jacob the thief, Jacob the deceiver, or Jacob the supplanter, the one who weaseled his way through life. He was now dubbed Sir Israel, prince with God, a shining knight of heroic resolve, one of resolute faith in the order of heaven, who struggled both with God and with man and prevailed.

Look at Genesis 32:31, a picture of Jacob walking away from the wrestling match with God. "He was limping because of his hip."

From that day forward and for the rest of his life, Jacob would limp. With every step, every time his name was called, he would be reminded that he was now a new man. The aged patriarch bore the perpetual marks of that wrestling match, a testament of his triumphant faith and renewed disposition in Christ.

Christ's meeting with you may not prove as dramatic. After all, it is not every day that a man gets to see the physical form of the Son of God. We don't all get to have an experience like the apostle Paul, who came face to face with Christ on the road to Damascus, got thrown off a horse, blinded by the light of His glory, and walked away to become the most powerful evangelist of all time.

Blinds, lames, prostitutes and lepers, hemorrhaging women, widows with dead sons, church officials with sick daughters, and political figures with dying servants of our day will not likely get an audience with Christ for Him to physically touch away their infirmities or send them home with reassuring words of deliverance. Not all of us will have such incredible tokens of our encounter with the King of glory. Yet all men and women of faith who are intimate with God, regardless of rank or social standing, bear the mark of such intimacy.

"To be a Christian," Martin Luther King Jr. says, "one must take up his cross, with all its difficulties and agonizing and tension-packed content, and carry it until that very cross leaves its mark upon us and redeems us to that more excellent way."

Faith leaves its mark indelibly etched into our characters: it leaves us looking and living like Christ.

PAINFUL TRANSFORMATION

ANYTHING worth doing will involves some measure of pain. Just ask a recovering addict trying to change his life, an accident survivor rehabilitating her body through physical therapy, or a teething baby. If your aim is to change your life, you can be sure the process will be painful.

The Christian life is one of never-ending trips to the crucible. Walking in the footsteps of the Man of Sorrows acquainted with grief, the God who became a Man and ended up dead in shame on the hills of the Place of the Skulls, often takes you through suffering, disappointments, and loss. Life with Christ is not for wimps. You cannot "make it" to heaven through a life of ease—not with the nature we have acquired through Adam. To prepare for cohabitation in paradise with a holy, righteous God, we need to see our sinful, wicked, hate-filled natures transformed into His likeness. That is a lifelong process, and demands lifelong pain.

Behind Enemy Lines

You and I were born on the wrong side of the cosmic conflict between God and His created archenemy, Satan. "Surely I was sinful at birth, sinful from the time my mother conceived me" David says (Psalm 51:5). We grew up on enemy territory, received our very natures from ancestors who themselves possessed sinful temperaments. Adam's choice in Eden determined the condition in which we are all born—our condition as enemies of God.

Because we were born and raised in this world, home of Satan and his army of infidels, who entertain themselves with evil experiments on human subjects, we turned out just like other victims of their exploitation. We, too, produced deeds of the world's system—deceit, selfishness, violence, greed, arrogance, adultery, envy, murder, etc. We, too, languished under the weight of sin and lawlessness, and became Exhibit A of all that is wrong with the world. But thank God for Jesus.

In the greatest rescue mission in the universe, the Son of God went into hostile territory behind enemy lines to extricate us from the firm grip of Satan. He came at one of the worst times in the history of humanity, amid murderous plots by both human and spiritual assassins, and proved that just because you live in a war-zone does not mean you have to be taken prisoner. His sinless life is a testimony that, regardless of the devil's allurements, you and I can live pure lives and can be upstanding citizens of heaven.

Because we had already acquired the habits and adopted the practices of God's enemies and because we had become addicted to the devil's drugs and had developed a penchant for his lifestyles, a change in character is paramount, hence the painful transformation.

Mind Surgery

Paul writes to the Romans, "I beseech you therefore, brethren, by the mercies of God, that you present your bodies a living sacrifice, holy, acceptable to God, which is your reasonable service. And do not be conformed to this world, but *be transformed by the renewing of your mind*, that you may prove what is that good and accept-able and perfect will of God" (Romans 12:1, 2, NKJV). He tells the Ephesians to "Put off, concerning your former conduct, the old man which grows corrupt according to the deceitful lusts, and *be renewed in the spirit of your mind*" (Ephesians 4:23, 24, NKJV).

Going from being the devil's lab rat to being a prince or princess in God's kingdom requires drastic changes. To think and speak and act like a man or woman after God's own heart, to change from our mentality of slave to that of a person whose citizenship is beyond the clouds at the Metropolis of the Universe necessitates "the renewing of your mind." We need a surgery, as it were—we need a mind transplant.

Transforming ourselves into the likeness of Christ is the personal renovation project of a lifetime. It is an arduous process that requires us daily to become living sacrifices, to deliberately give ourselves to God, put forth strenuous efforts to reject, abandon, and avoid sin. That's no simple task. It can be frustrating as after years of struggle we look over our lives and realize that our efforts have brought us no closer to our goals. But regardless of how difficult it is, Paul urges us with great emotion to do it.

Mind renewal requires us first to perform a voluntary act of surrender. We must willingly relinquish ourselves to God: mind and heart, time and talents, possessions and intellectual acuities. We choose to bring to Him all that we are, place ourselves upon the altar to Him as living sacrifices. We must also make the hard choice not to conform.

Conformity is easy. When the tides of evil press against us on all sides, when everywhere we turn we see evidence of depravity, when culture presents dissoluteness in pretty packages of freedom and pleasure, it takes nothing to let our guards down and jump in headfirst for a swim in the pool of degeneracy, to conform to the lifestyles and vices of those around us. It takes discipline, strength of heart and mind, and a truckload of God's grace to daily keep from giving in to the allurements of society. The world offers many "freedoms" that, if indulged, will usurp God's place as the anchor of our lives. We must deliberately refuse to give in; we must refuse to conform at all costs.

Instead we are called to be transformed—by the renewing of our minds.

Sin is planned and executed in the mind before we ever see evidence of it. Being the seat of our intellect, the place of thought and reasoning, every single act that we commit is first manufactured on the production lines of our minds. A renewal of the person must also involve a renewal of the mind. Commenting on 1 Peter 1:13, 14 Chuck Swindoll writes, "Holiness starts in the mind. It includes a departure from ignorance and a renewal of your thought life. And it leads to conforming to Christ's holiness rather than to the lusts of the world."[58] This departure from ignorance and thought-life renewal may necessitate extreme measures.

In His Sermon on the Mount, Christ prescribes radical remedies for mind renewal. "'If your right eye causes you to sin, gouge it out and throw it away,'" He said. "'And if your right hand causes you to sin, cut it off and throw it away'" (Matthew 5:29, 30).

There are things in our lives, certain habits and practices, that have become so much a part of who we are that breaking them requires drastic measures, uncompromising approaches. These habits can only be removed through the grueling process of amputation.

You will need a change in scenery to change certain habits. Others will demand that you give up favorite activities and practices. You may have to sever ties with some very close friends or family members, or part ways with a lucrative career, or withdraw membership from a preferred social club, or abandon a favorite pastime. According to Christ nothing is off limits. Members of your body, if that is what it takes—things that are part of your temperament—may have to be amputated if they present a hindrance to your faith.

In addition to fleeing known sins and breaking bad habits, mind renewal also requires purposeful, calculated study of God's Word. The Psalmist wonders, "How can a young man keep his way pure?" *How do I do this thing called holiness? How do I keep from conforming, from becoming like the people whose light I am called to become?* He readily finds the answer, "By living according to your word!" (Psalm 119:9).

Careful study of God's Word, which is able to penetrate "even to dividing soul and spirit, joints and marrow," with the power to judge "the thoughts and attitudes of the heart" (Hebrews 4:12), is necessary to renew, regenerate, and rejuvenate our minds. We need daily portions—morning, noon, and evening; breakfast, lunch, and dinner; and sometimes snack-sized bites—of God's Word if our characters are to be transformed into the character of Jesus; this is not an easy thing to do, especially in our day and age.

Abandoning sin is extremely difficult for men and women whose real sense of right and wrong is tainted by a society whose idea of fun often involves humiliation, adultery, casual sex, rape, and human cruelty in the form of reality TV, video games, and movies. The transition to becoming a man or woman after God's own heart is a project that requires the losing of our lives, that demands an investment of blood, sweat, and tears.

We will sometimes hate the person staring back at us in the mirror, realizing how ugly we are in our sins, how much of a failure we must be in the eyes of heaven. To make it to the end will require dramatic changes in focus from self to God. And we are urged to do it, to beat our bodies and make them our slaves.

We are urged to even embrace the death of our mortal bodies, because it will be worth it. For when the dust settles, when the books are opened and names are called, the rewards of that transformed life will transcend our wildest dreams. It will be "a crown that will last forever" (1 Corinthians 9:25); what we gain in the end will be things that no eyes have seen and no ears have heard, things that have never been conceived by men.

May we purify our hearts, renew our minds, and transform our bodies and our characters, no matter how painful the process proves to be, in order to receive that crown.

GOD PLACED A BET

IT all began when God gathered His "sons," members of His heavenly administration, together for what might as well have been a staff meeting. For some reason the devil, who was not necessarily invited, felt the urge to crash the party. God singled him out and struck up a conversation, taking the opportunity to brag a little.

"Where've you been, Satan?" God asked.

"O, here and there, up and down the earth, prowling around, looking for victims."

"Have you considered My servant Job?" God asked, knowing the details of the devil's heart, what he desired to do to Job, as if to say, *Here is a potential target.*

The devil lost it. He made the case that Job's piety was inspired by wrong motives. "Yeah, right!" he said sardonically. "You mean to tell me Job doesn't have any incentive for serving You? Look at the man! Look at the size of his bank account. Look at his wife and kids. Look at his businesses. Any man in his position has causes to praise and worship! You build an impenetrable wall of protection around everything he has; I can't even look at him without legions of Your angels getting in my face, threatening to burn my tail!

"But I bet if You, take away the riches and the beautiful children—let him squirm a little—then You will hear from Job how he truly feels about You. He will curse You to Your face!"

What a challenge!

The devil was attacking God's judgment, implying that His assessment of Job's character was erroneous. The man was not really faithful out of love but out of greed. Satan insinuated that the problem is really with God, who entices people to "love" Him through bribery. He pulls the strings of protection and material possessions and, like puppets, people respond with their allegiance.

Satan *guaranteed* that, should God allow him to have his way with Job, shake him up a little, Job's allegiance would prove to be a sham.

I imagine the creatures present at the meeting watched in suspenseful anticipation, anxious to hear what God would say next. Would He agree to the bet? Would He stake His reputation on a shaky, unreliable human being? Or would He simply allow the devil to walk away with satisfaction, knowing that he had caused the God of the universe to eat His own Words?

God loves a good challenge; impossibility seems to be one of His specialties. He loves to reveal the unknowable, and appears quick to rise to the occasion whenever there is hopelessness and impossible odds, because His power is made perfect in hopelessness. So He decided to prove the falsity of the devil's claims and make it clear before men, angels, the adversary himself, and all other inhabitants of the universe, that men *can* (and some *do*) serve God out of love and not from ulterior motives.

I'll take your bet, God told the enemy. "I'm leaving all he has in your hands to do with as you please. But don't you touch the man himself."

I have the benefit of knowing the end of the story, yet I tremble at the prospect of what might have happened if Job had failed. God put His character on the line! As Philip Yancey observes, there was an arm wrestling match between Satan and God, and God "designated the man Job to be his stand-in,"[59] pegging His unchangeable Word, the very foundation of the universe—without which the entire order of creation would simply disintegrate—to the responses of one frail human being, and in the process risking the ultimate failure of His Word.

The Assailed One

Every year, *Forbes* magazine assembles the cast of the wealthiest people on the planet and publishes this data under the heading

"The World's Billionaires." The 2016 list had 1,810 billionaires, with a total net worth of $6.5 trillion!*

Atop the billionaire list is Microsoft co-founder Bill Gates, with a net worth of $75 billion. At number two is Spain's Amancio Ortega, worth $67 billion. American Warren Buffet is at number three with just under $61 billion. Mexican businessman Carlos Slim Helu is at number four, with a net worth of $50 billion, and Amazon.com founder Jeff Bezos rounds off the top five with a net worth of just over $45 billion.

If *Forbes* magazine was around during the patriarchal period, I imagine that the most famous man in the land of Uz would have made that list a few times. He was, after all, the greatest man of the East. Since in those days wealth was not measured in stocks and bonds and bank ledgers, we do not know for sure how many billions Job might have been worth. What we do know is, in terms of livestock and crops, servants, and other business ventures, Job had no equal. Chuck Swindoll commented that Job would probably be worth more than Bill Gates, Donald Trump and Ross Perot combined. However, I sense that Job's net worth was not simply measured by his sizable wealth. His greatness had more to do with character than it did with material possessions.

The brief profile of the man, as recorded in the first five verses of the book that bears his name, uses four key terms to describe him that we do not typically find in the biographies of today's business moguls.

First, Job was "perfect" (KJV). His perfection implied a spiritual relationship with God that stayed within the confines of His requirements. As a Christian today, Job would have done what his conscience and the Word of God convicted him was right.

Second, Job was upright. He was not crooked, did not portray

* As of March 1, 2016

something he actually was not. He was "straight," a man who strove to do right by everyone. Job was fair in his business dealings, and would not cut corners to earn an extra million dollars. He was the same man whether he was at the synagogue, in the bedroom, at the ballpark, or on the pulpit.

Third, Job "feared God." People fear many things these days: diseases, death, job loss, not being able to make the rent; we are crippled by our fears. This kind of fear does not express Job's sentiment toward God. His was a reverential awe that stemmed from his high esteem of his Lord. It drove him to acknowledge God's sovereignty, power, and authority as his Maker.

Finally, Job "shunned evil." This was a man who did not play with sin. The idea here is to run away from evil, avoid it as though it were a contagious, incurable disease. Job literally ran away from sin. He would not pause for a second look, or ponder what might have been when temptation presented itself. Instead he purposefully endeavored to please his God and stay in harmony with Him—not an easy thing to do in any society.

Job was not the kind of rich man whose integrity and family became collateral damage to his wealth. He was not a licentious skirt chaser with three divorces under his belt and a litany of mistresses. Job loved his wife and children. He was pure as a man, faithful as a husband, caring as a father. He was a man's man, a man whose love and care and passion for his family far outweighed his concerns for wealth.

Not that his children were party animals or drunkards, but people can be careless and say or do things that they should not when engaged in fun and leisurely activities. So Job took the time to pray for his seven grown sons and three grown daughters whenever they got together to hang out, in case they forgot themselves and said or did something out of line. That's the kind of man Job was.

Then came verse 13.

Job's very name is a testament to the events that plagued his life. It is from the Hebrew *'Iyyob*, which means "the assailed one," a name Bible commentators believe was possibly given to Job after the events in the book that bears his name. The man saw his life shattered to pieces, completely leveled to the ground. In a matter of moments he went from a picture of wealth and prosperity to the epitome of misfortune.

Having gotten the green light from God, Satan unleashed his devilish best against Job. The man had no time to breathe or think between severe blows, and with each blow his case seemed more hopeless. The messengers came to him one after the other bearing horrendous news that constantly intensified, beginning with the oxen and donkeys being stolen, to the sheep being burned up, to the camels being raided, and culminating with his children—all ten of them, seven sons and three daughters—being killed in one day.

I personally find Job 1:16 disturbing, where the messenger suggests that "'the fire of God fell from heaven and burned up the sheep and the servants!'" *God did it, Job! The God you dedicate your entire life to; the God you serve with unwavering staunchness and unreserved loyalty; He turned on you!* (Job himself would attribute his misfortune to God [Job 2:10; 6:3]).

Job's response to his trials has brought me to tears. The record shows that, having heard of the day's events, after however long it took Job to absorb the news, he got up, tore up his robe, shaved his head, fell to the ground, and worshipped.

He got up because the news must have knocked him down. I imagine Job prostrate on the floor, banging his fists against the dirt, wailing for his dead grown children.

Then he tore his robe, a gesture performed by people in intense, horrifying grief, sorrow, or disappointment (Genesis 37:34; 1 Kings

21:27). By this action Job was saying, *My heart is overwhelmed with bitter anguish!*

Next, Job shaved his head, another demonstration of his sorrowful ordeal. It was a sign of shame and loss of glory (see Isaiah 15:2). Everything he enjoyed in life, it seems, was taken away.

These are the normal responses to grief; they are what I would expect Job to have done. His next action is what confuses me; I am shocked by what I read next in verse 20: Job fell back to the ground, this time not to express sorrow, not to announce to the world his depthless grief, not to challenge God to a bout, but to *worship!*

I think of my responses when the budget does not quite meet the requirements of my bills, how I react when I pray for something and do not get an answer, when another driver cuts me off or when someone "disrespects" me. I often find myself angry, sometimes even throwing a fit, blaming others, questioning God.

Yet there was this righteous, "perfect" man who did everything right, of whom the holy, righteous God Himself declared "'there is no one on earth like him'" on account of his blamelessness. He went bankrupt, lost his fortune, and buried *all of his ten grown children in one day!* If anyone had reason to demand of God, "Why are You picking on me?" it was Job. Instead of clinching his teeth, shaking his fist in God's face demanding "How dare you?!" he stripped himself of his clothes, dropped down to his knees, arms hanging loose to his sides, and worshipped!

It sends shockwaves down my spine.

Job seemed to realize something that we would do well to remember in our worst moments of trial: It's not about us. God is not here to cater to our whims. He is not up there in the heavens for our comfort. Rather, *we* are made for His glory. Our wellbeing, suffering, success and failure, pleasure and pain—everything that we face in this life, every opportunity we are afforded, must somehow pay dividends to God in the form of glory. Our lives, whether lived in the pit or on the mountaintop, must bring Him praise, honor, and worship.

Job understood this much, dropped to the floor a miserable wretch as he said, I imagine with tears in his eyes, "'Naked I came from my mother's womb, and naked I will depart. The Lord gave and the Lord has taken away; may the name of the Lord be praised!'"

Round One was over; the devil lost. In my mind's eye I can see him in a corner, sulking and cursing Job. His charges against God and Job had proved untrue. God was right after all; Job's worship was not motivated by greed. He loved God simply because God is God, simply because that is the whole duty of man (Ecclesiastes 12:13). The Lord won the bet, and all of heaven applauded.

Hitting Rock Bottom

The events of Job's life to this point contained enough adversity to last ten lifetimes. Few men would stand for a second round after taking so many blows. But Job had not reached the nadir of despair. Not yet. He was just about to learn what it means to go through the crucible, to drink Satan's fury down to the very last dregs.

We do not know how much time elapsed between Job's first and second tests, but while he reeled from deep loss, God called another staff meeting, and the devil crashed the party again.

God singled him out and exercised His bragging rights.

"'Have you considered my servant Job? *There is no one on earth like him!*'"

I love it!

God was saying, *Look at the man! He is still maintaining his integrity, still a man of his word, still My trophy of a servant, the greatest man of the East, even though* "'you incited me against him to ruin him without any reason!'" *The man stands his ground,*

Satan; he still maintains his allegiance to Me. I was right; I am always right! I won the bet!

Satan's response shows the kind of inconsistency you can always expect from the devil. The truth is whatever suits him at the moment, and his series of lies seem to always accompany some guarantee. He makes promises he cannot keep, or as a pastor once put it, Satan "writes checks that his character cannot cash."

In the first meeting he guaranteed God that, by allowing him to assail Job he would "surely curse you to your face" (Job 1:11). And although he had been forced to swallow his words, Satan maintained that Job's allegiance was bogus.

"Skin for skin!" he snapped. *The man surely has his price. I may have been wrong about his business, wealth, and family, but I bet You he'd fold if You took his health and dignity. Make him suffer undeservedly; have a few friends misunderstand and accuse him of wrongdoing; turn the ones he loves most against him, and I promise You,* "he will surely curse You to Your face!"

Again God responded, "I'll take your bet! Go at Job; give him your best shot. Torture him to the utmost, strike the man to your evilest best. Simply preserve his life."

I must again reiterate how the story of Job disturbs me. Even as I pray for God to help me become a man of outrageous faith, I grapple with the idea of God standing by while I get thumped. Not only did God Himself suggest Job to the devil, He then stood by and allowed the man to get thrashed half to death. How could He just sit there while Satan literally destroyed the life of not only an innocent man but also His prized trophy of a servant? Shouldn't He have done something? Job's story makes me realize that, in many of my trials, God seems like a bystander, watching on the sideline, refusing to interfere.

Two things in the story bring me comfort.

First, even in His supposed inaction, God limits the devil's power. In the first contest he could only take away Job's "stuff"— he was not allowed to touch the man himself—and in the second, he was not permitted to take Job's life.

Second, as Philip Yancey observes, Job's trials were not about pain. The unfair shellacking he received had everything to do with God's reputation before the unseen world. Job was God's chosen chess piece, His weapon of choice to win in the great struggle against the forces of darkness. He was, in Yancey's words, "God's Exhibit A, his demonstration piece to the powers of the unseen world."

This brings me some comfort because it helps me realize that God does not waste calamities. When we are struck down doing our best to follow His leading, when in the middle of trying to live a blameless life tragedies strike, it may just be that God had selected us to settle a score with Satan! This is a sobering thought for me, as I am often a complainer. It only means that I am running away, rejecting God's choice of me as His stand-in. I pray that God helps me to represent Him with as much class as Job did.

Again the devil left God's presence and charged against Job with full force.

While the man was down, thinking life could not possibly get any worse, he realized that what he had suffered thus far was a walk in the park. Immediately, Satan "struck Job with painful boils from the sole of his foot to the crown of his head" (Job 2:7).

Job was hit with a rare inflammatory disease. His appearance was completely transformed as the surface of his entire body was covered with painful sores. His body was deformed; his face barely recognizable, and pain ravaged his rotten flesh at wildfire intensity. Job couldn't escape his own stench, and he watched in disgust as repugnant eruptions seeped from the boils.

In *Job*, the seventh book of his "Great Lives" series, Chuck

Swindoll puts together a list of the symptoms that Job suffered as a result of the ulcerous boils that broke out on him. Among them he listed "purulent sores that burst open, scab over, crack, and ooze with pus"; "a darkening of one eyelid"; weight loss; foul breath; "degenerative changes in facial skin, disfiguration"; difficulty breathing; persistent itching; "high fever with chills and discoloring of skin as well as anxiety and diarrhea"; "excruciating, continual pain." Job's condition, Swindoll writes, resulted in rejection and isolation. He became so deplorable that he was removed from society and relocated to the city dump. "It was the place where they burned garbage and human excrement from the city. This became his place of existence."[60]

To me Job 2:8 paints the sorriest picture of the man. Dazed and isolated, Job held a piece of pottery in his hands, scraping himself to remove the puss oozing from his sores. This was how low God's perfect servant had fallen. Job reached the lowermost of all lows, and that cracked open to let the man fall lower still.

Misunderstood by His Wife

It is one thing to be the victim of circumstances, to have everything in life working against you. It is something entirely different when it appears that everyone you love, everyone you know, either misunderstands you or turns on you. Job had come to such a point in his life.

Satan was not content to simply take the man's his health, his comfort, and his dignity. He also managed to successfully, at least on the surface, turn all the people whom Job loved and respected against him. It began with Job's wife.

Up to this point Job's wife had been silent. She seemed to have remained in the background, to have suffered on the sidelines. But before the arrival of his friends, Job had had a run-in with his wife.

This was a woman who no doubt loved and respected her

husband, and don't forget that she, too, had lost all of her fortune. She had gone from being one of the most respected women in the country to a mere peasant. Through it all she kept her emotions under wrap, stayed in the margins. She was not a loud, quarrelsome, vulgar woman. She behaved herself as a graceful, God-fearing woman, but she, too, had her limits.

It was one thing to have lost all of her belongings; she managed to cope with *burying her ten grown children in one day!* But now she was watching as her husband's body literally festered and deteriorated while he was still alive. This proved to be more than Mrs. Job could bear. She could no longer manage the fire scorching in the deepest depth of her soul, would rather see Job die than suffer this indignity. In her eyes he did not deserve it; at least death would be more honorable. This, I believe, was the vantage point from which Job's wife spoke. This was an angry woman in deep emotional turmoil; she simply had had enough.

"Are you still maintaining your integrity?" Mrs. Job snapped. *What good is it for you to be righteous? God has forgotten about you! He forgets to show mercy, forgets the righteous while He caters to the wicked who thrives in his wickedness. God has no time to bother with you, Job! Don't you get it? Why don't you just give it up?* "Curse God and die!"

Job saw trough her frustration and responded kindly. Listen to his answer. "You are *talking like a foolish woman*" he said. "Shall we accept good from God, and not trouble?" Job was not suggesting that his wife was foolish. Rather, he was saying that she sounded like our version of prosperity gospel preachers, who promise a nice and behaving god who never does anything to get under our skin, a god who simply blesses and never curses. But that's not the God that Job served.

Job's wife misunderstood him, and she misunderstood God. She

176

thought that faith put God under a contract where He was now obliged to make everything go according to her plan: keep her children healthy, put food on the table, keep milk in the ice box, and dollars in the bank. And like Mrs. Job, many of us get it wrong today.

Job's response was direct and to the point. God is not obliged to regularly bless us. The same way He blesses, He can also allow curse. He is sovereign and worthy of worship regardless of what He chooses to do. God has not lost His ability to be good and compassionate because the bottom has fallen from under us. To the contrary you will find out, often in retrospect, that on some of your worst days God had proven Himself most faithful.

Censured by His Friends
"When Job's three friends, Eliphaz the Temanite, Bildad the Shuhite and Zophar the Naamathite, heard about all the troubles that had come upon him, they set out from their homes and met together by agreement to go and sympathize with him and comfort him" (Job 2:11).

Job's friends had noble intentions. They had come to comfort him in the grimmest, direst moment of his existence. When they saw Job from a distance they did not even recognize their friend, who had metamorphosed into a monstrous creature. Looking at his condition, they simply could not take it. They "raised their voices and wept" (Job 2:12, NKJV). Those grown men wailed like children, poured out their souls to express grief for their friend. Then they tore their robes, the same manner in which Job expressed his grief, and threw dusts over their heads. Eliphaz, Bildad, and Zophar sat on the ground next to Job in silence for seven days and nights without speaking one word to him! Not one of them opened his mouth to address Job until Job broke his own silence.

Unfortunately, they did finally speak, and that's when the problems began.

For thirty-four chapters, Job's friends hammered away at him nonstop in what turned out to be three rounds of debates. It began with Eliphaz, possibly the oldest of the bunch, then Bildad, then Zophar, with Elihu, the youngest of them all, taking the last six chapters. Job answered them one after the other. When each round was over, they began the blame game all over again.

God declared Job upright and perfect, a man who feared God and shunned evil; his friends disagreed. They maintained that nobody suffers undeservedly. "'Who, being innocent, has ever perished?'" Eliphaz began. "'Where were the upright ever destroyed? As I have observed, those who plow evil and those who sow trouble reap it. At the breath of God they are destroyed; at the blast of his anger they perish'" (Job 4:7–9). He encouraged Job to appeal to God and beg forgiveness for his sins.

After Job's response to Eliphaz, Bildad came against him with full force. *Come on, Job,* he says. *Are you kidding me? If your kids sinned, God delivered them to their own transgressions. But if you would simply pray and ask forgiveness, God would show up right now and restore your estate.*

Does this sound familiar? That's because many today preach this same gospel. They declare that suffering only comes to those who are living outside of God's will. Bildad insisted that Job only suffered because he had some secret sin; he lost his kids because they were sinners, and he would continue to suffer until he begged for God's forgiveness.

"'Can papyrus grow tall where there is no marsh?'" Bildad wondered aloud. "'While still growing and uncut, they wither more quickly than grass. Such is the destiny of all who forget God; so perishes the hope of the godless. What he trusts in is fragile; what he relies on is a spider's web. He leans on his web, but it gives way;

he clings to it, but it does not hold'" (Job 8:11–15). *Job, if you don't turn to God, everything in nature will turn against you!*

Job responded to Bildad, but as soon as he stopped speaking Zophar came in like a storm.

Your self-righteous rants won't silence us, Job. You keep telling God that you are wise before Him; I wish God would just open His mouth and answer you. You claim to be righteous; He has even forgotten some of your sins. Give it up, Job. Throw yourself at God's mercy and admit you've sinned!

"'If you devote your heart to him and stretch out your hands to him, if you put away the sin that is in your hand and allow no evil to dwell in your tent, then you will lift up your face without shame; you will stand firm and without fear. You will surely forget your trouble, recalling it only as waters gone by'" (Job 11:13-15).

With each discourse, which seems longer than his friends' accusations, Job relentlessly rejected their notion that he was suffering because of some hidden sins. But they pressed on him, insisting that he was guilty. At some point Job grew tired of their rumblings and told them exactly how he felt about them.

Easy for you to say! he snapped. "'Men at ease have contempt for misfortune'" (Job 12:5). I like how the New American Standard Bible expresses this truth that Job had for his friends: "'Sorry comforters are you all!'" (Job 16:2).

Job called his friends "'worthless physicians'" who "'smear me with lies,'" and wished that they would simply put a sock in it. "'If only you would be altogether silent! For you, that would be wisdom'" (Job 13:4, 5). *Shut your mouth and be counted as wise!* "'Your memorable sayings are proverbs of ashes, your defenses are defenses of clay'" (verse 12, NASB).

Forgotten by His God

It is from his speeches to his friends that we truly learn the depth of Job's calamity. In poetic language, words well understood because they are so relevant to our time, Job expounds the degree to which he is assailed.

Job worshiped God in his trouble (Job 1:20, 21). He defended God (2:10) and kept silence before Him (2:13). Throughout his ordeal the man harbored no ill feeling toward his Maker or his fellowmen. He moaned and groaned without sinning, spent at least a full week in dreadful silence during which he must have contemplated his circumstances, delved the deepest depth of his soul, and searched for answers. Job must have taken the time to overanalyze his life, trying to see where he went wrong, what he said or did to warrant such severe punishment—for that is what he felt he was receiving: cruel, unmerited punishment. But nothing came up, not a word ill spoken, not the mistreatment of a friend or enemy, yet here he was in excruciating pain.

Feeling his body literally ripping to shreds, suffering sleeplessness, loneliness, neglect and a host of other calamities, Job finally asked the question that most of us would have asked upon first being confronted by the devil: "Why me?"

He began by cursing the day of his birth, cursing his conception, and cursing his survival as a baby. He then begged for death, which would offer rest from labor and suffering, and in death he would share the company of the greats of all time who had preceded him to the grave.

Job complained about the degree of his pain, which robbed him of his sleep and turned his nights into long, interminable journeys. "'The churning inside me never stops'" he laments; "'days of suffering confront me. I go about blackened, but not by the sun; I stand up in the assembly and cry for help. I have become a brother of jackals, a companion of owls. My skin grows black and peels; my body burns with fever'" (Job 30:27–30). He had become "'nothing but skin and bones; I have escaped only by the skin of my teeth'" (Job 19:20).

Job then turned his attention toward God, whom he felt was picking on him. He felt "the arrows of the Almighty are within me; their poison my spirit drinks; the terrors of God are arrayed against me!" (Job 6:4, NASB). "'All was well with me, but he shattered me; he seized me by the neck and crushed me. He has made me his target; his archers surround me. Without pity, he pierces my kidneys and spills my gall on the ground. Again and again he bursts upon me; he rushes at me like a warrior'" (Job 16:12–14).

In his book *A Grief Observed* C. S. Lewis explains that when your case seems most hopeless, God often seems farthest away.

"When you are happy, so happy that you have no sense of needing Him...if you remember yourself and turn to Him with gratitude and praise, you will be—or so it feels—welcomed with open arms. But go to Him when your need is desperate, when all other help is vain, and what do you find? A door slammed in your face, and a sound of bolting and double bolting on the inside. After that, silence. You may as well turn away. The longer you wait, the more emphatic the silence will become."[61]

What proves most unbearable to Job throughout his ordeal was God's emphatic silence.

It might have been easier for Job to endure the ordeal had he known why. I believe that Job would have proudly represented God, would have been more than honored to be a stand-in for the Lord Almighty, had he known that his suffering would bring Him glory, that his pain would help settle the issues of the great controversy.

But the man was kept in the dark. As far as he could tell, God rolled the newspaper, squashed him like a mosquito, and then walked away from him, taking along with His presence all that was precious. The questions went unanswered; his pleas were ignored. This was what frustrated Job most.

"'Why do you hide your face and consider me your enemy?'" (Job 13:24). "'If only I knew where to find him; if only I could go to his dwelling! I would state my case before him and fill my mouth with arguments. I would find out what he would answer me, and consider what he would say'" (Job 23:3-5). "'I cry out to you, O God, but you do not answer; I stand up, but you merely look at me'" (Job 30:20).

Job longs for God to break His silence, and becomes frustrated when He does not. The longer the silence lingers the more he talks, and the more self-righteous he becomes. He sounds proud in his speeches, and the rants ring closer and closer to blasphemy as he pounds away at God demanding answers.

Rejected by All Others

Now Job laments the treatment he received from others. The greatest man of the East, on account of both his integrity and wealth was now viewed with ridicule by friends and strangers alike. His circumstances appalled him.

"'I am a joke to my friends, the one who called on God and He answered him; the just and blameless man is a joke'" (Job 12:4, NASB). People who were guests in Job's house no longer treated him as the head of the household, as provider and breadwinner. Even his servants, whose livelihoods his hard earned cash provided for, ignored him. They no longer treated him with respect; they simply refused to come when he called on them. "'I summon my servant, but he does not answer, though I beg him with my own mouth.'" Because of the disease his breath was foul and offensive to his wife (Job 19:13–17).

Young children, who in that era recognized the respect due to the aged, scorned Job. "'When I appear, they ridicule me.'" It had gotten to the point where even the most debased in his society saw Job's distress as an opportunity to insult him. "'Those younger than I mock me, whose fathers I disdained to put with the dogs of my flock.'" "'And now I have become their taunt, I have even become a byword to them. They abhor me and stand aloof of me, and *they do not refrain from spitting at my face!*'" (Job 19:18, 19; 30:1, 9, 10, NASB).

Can you imagine falling to that low? Job's calamity is unparalleled. I believe that the only other sufferer in Scripture who endured more shame, more pain, more humiliation than Job is Christ. The devil was determined to bring him down, and threw everything he had at the man—not just the kitchen sink, but the whole kitchen. The assaults came in all shapes and sizes. And by all accounts it seemed as though God was behind it. What was Job to do?

Though He Slay Me

In *David*, the first book of his "Great Lives" series, Chuck Swindoll writes: "When the sovereign God brings us to nothing, it is to reroute our lives, not to end them."[62] Job must have known this. He weighed his options, looked at his life, and considered what to do. Everything around him seemed to indicate that God was the enemy, the oppressor who ground his life to powder. Yet in spite of God's apparent assaults, Job made up his mind to trust Him anyway. "Job weighed the evidence, most of which did not suggest a trusting God. But he decided, kicking and screaming all the way, to place his faith in God."[63]

"'I know that my Redeemer lives, and that in the end he will stand upon the earth. And after my skin has been destroyed, yet in my flesh I will see God; I myself will see him with my own eyes—I, and not another. How my heart yearns within me!'" (Job 19:25–27).

In spite of my pain, Job says, *God is sitting up there on His* throne. *Good or bad, life or death, in gladness or calamity, God is still God. And God is still good. My Redeemer lives! And after all of this is over, when He returns in glory to save the righteous, I will see Him with my own eyes!*

In the meantime I'll just hold onto to God. While He beats my body to the dust, I will trust Him, I will love Him still. Though worms break out on my body, ulcers seeping puss flow down my legs, pain ravaging my flesh, still I will put my hope in His goodness. Yes, I will reel in pain; I will groan under the weight of my calamities. As is common to men, I will shed tears of sorrows and mourn my sorry state. But never in my life *will I give up on my God. Never!* "'Though He slay me, yet will I trust Him!'" (Job 13:15, NKJV).

According to Swindoll, this scene played out while Job was still sitting in the city dump surrounded by garbage and burnt human waste. But Job looked beyond it to the ultimate will of his God. "I will come forth as gold!"

After what must have been months of intense suffering Job finally received what people who suffer long for but have never been granted and probably never will: a personal visit from God.

It's None of Your Business

Following the three rounds of debate and Elihu's spectacular six-chapter rebuttal, God storms onto the scene to put an end to the debate. But instead of providing answers, He came to Job with more questions.

Who do you think you are? God asked Job. *Who is this fool who speaks ignorantly of things he does not understand? Man up, Job! I'm going to teach you a thing or two!* Then on the Lord went, ultimately telling Job, until you've created and run your own universe, don't you dare tell Me how to run Mine.

To challenge Job God called forth the magnificence of His creative genius in planting the foundations of the earth, deciding on its measurements, designing its borders and setting in motion its rules. Then He questioned him concerning the ocean, which He treated as a baby that bursts from the womb, a baby He then wrapped in soft clouds, tucked away within its confines as a mother puts a child in a playpen, saying to it "'Thus far you shall come, but no farther'" (Job 38:11, NASB).

As God's four-chapter monologue progressed, with a couple of minor interruptions from Job, He summoned His power over the created universe to demand that *Job* answer to *Him*. In the first two chapters (38 and 39) He called up the dawn, light, darkness, snow, hail, floods, rain, lightning, thunder, ice, frost, dew, clouds, stars, and the animal kingdom.

Trembling, I imagine, with his hands over his mouth, Job had no choice but to admit, "'I'm speechless, in awe—words fail me. I should never have opened my mouth! I've talked too much, way too much. *I'm ready to shut up and listen*'" (Job 40:3–5, MSG).

But God would not let Job off that easily.

"How dare you challenge My judgment to justify yourself? Why don't you try being God for a moment? Go ahead, save yourself, tell Me how that works out for you! Do you have a booming bass of a voice like Mine? Do you have arms strong like Mine, possess a panoramic view of past, present and future as I do? Can you manage the world as I do? Why don't you try dealing with the wicked, punishing his sins, bringing him down when he had gone too far? Once you possess attributes like Mine—glory and splendor, honor and majesty—to run the world better than Me, then I will back down and declare that you, Job, can save yourself. Until then, shut your mouth and let God be God!" (Job 40:8–14, paraphrased).

God offered no apology, no explanation, no encouraging words.

In my view this is God's answer to Job's "Why me?" question, if you could call it an answer: "It's none of your business!"

God was saying to Job, in effect, *What I do with My creation is My business, not yours, even when it reduces your life to a pile of rubble!* In the end, God did not bother to answer any of Job's charges, or his friends' charges for that matter.

And Job got it! Listen to his response. "'I babbled on about things far beyond me, made small talk about wonders way over my head.... I admit I once lived by rumors of you; now I have it all firsthand—from my own eyes and ears! I'm sorry—forgive me. I'll never do that again, I promise! I'll never again live on crusts of hearsay, crumbs of rumor'" (Job 42:3–6, MSG).

LAST WORDS
Bearing the Mark

JOB'S story concludes in a way we can all appreciate. God restored everything that Job lost, and then some. Job became twice as rich, twice as influential. The businesses were twice as successful as before; Job even had ten brand new children—seven sons and three daughters. But before rushing to celebrate, take a moment to consider the man and what he had become.

Job's first ten children were all grown. As Swindoll observes, he had no diapers to change, no baths to give, no carpools, no big meals to prepare, no lunches for school, no teenage daughters with nose rings and pierced bellybuttons, and no boys with big tattoos. Job had been there, done that, and had no plans to start over, no desire to go through those cycles again.

But after his suffering there was Job again, going through sleepless nights feeding and pacing with fussing babies who refused to sleep. Remember that it takes nine months to produce a baby. So Job needed to wait at least ten years to get his children back, even if he had them one year apart (assuming no twins or triplets). Furthermore, no parent simply forgets a child that they bury. The memories of those first grown boys and girls, who may have had their own families, must have haunted Job's sleep for the rest of his life.

Also, anybody who has ever declared bankruptcy knows that it is painfully difficult to climb out of it. While I believe that Providence was on Job's side, and that "all his brothers and sisters and everyone who had known him before came...and each one gave him a piece of silver and a gold ring" (Job 42:11), he could not have built his fortune overnight. For the greatest man of the East to become twice as great as before, he must have put in some long hours.

In the end, I believe that the greatest mark left in the wake of Job's trials is a higher consciousness and greater notion of God. The man after the process was not the man before. This Job learned that God can always be trusted, even when the very things He does stand in stark contrast to all that we know about Him. No man can be the same who has come to the end of his rope, who has had no one to lean on but God, who had borne his cross to the point that the cross itself has crushed him. Because in the end, after riding the tides of adversity, drinking the gall of misery to its very dregs, suffering the worst that life has to offer and *still* hold on to his God, he comes through strong as oak, purified as gold, solid as a rock. Job reached the point where his intimacy with God resulted in a faith that could never again be shaken. "Faith like Job's cannot be shaken because it is the result of being shaken" Rabbi Abraham Heschel says.

Job never got an answer to his "why me?" questions...or did he?

Was the answer God's presence? Was the answer the realization that God is sovereign, omniscient, omnipotent, and good...*no matter what?* Was the answer "trust God at all cost!"?

Job seemed content in the end, and repented in dust and ashes.

When it was all said and done he was left with a faith that few other men can boast of—a pit-refined, crucible-tested faith that no amount of suffering could erode, a faith that says God is worthy of trust, and the privilege of knowing Him is worth enduring the worst this life has to offer!

9

THE END OF OUR FAITH

"THEN I SAW in the right hand of him who sat on the throne a scroll with writing on both sides and sealed with seven seals," Revelation 5 begins. "And I saw a mighty angel proclaiming in a loud voice, 'Who is worthy to break the seals and open the scroll?' But no one in heaven or on earth or under the earth could open the scroll or even look inside it. I wept and wept because no one was found who was worthy to open the scroll or look inside. Then one of the elders said to me, 'Do not weep! See, *the Lion of the tribe of Judah, the Root of David, has triumphed. He is able to open the scroll and its seven seals*'" (Revelation 5:1–5).

No one is good enough.

No one qualifies.

No exception!

This, according to Paul, is the case of every breathing soul who walks the face of planet earth. Here he is, addressing the Romans: "'There is no one righteous, not even one; there is no one who understands, no one who seeks God. All have turned away, they have together become worthless; there is no one who does good, not even one'" (Romans 3:10–12).

No matter who you are, how much you have done or may be doing for God, by your own merit you fail the righteousness test. In the end, Isaiah tells us, the verdict is the same: "We are all as an unclean thing, and all our righteousnesses are as filthy rags" (Isaiah 64:6, KJV).

Survey the lives of history's greats. Review the records of Scripture's worthies. Go into the Hall of Faith and pull the files on the greatest men and women who ever lived. You will find little foxes that spoiled their vines, dead flies in their ointments. Even those whose records remain spotless—men like Enoch and Daniel—when compared to the standard of God's perfect righteousness, even these fall short. The question is, How can a man stand before God and claim righteousness? How can you and I ever hit the mark?

A single, five-letter word meets the challenge: F-A-I-T-H! Thank God for Jesus, through faith in Him, we can stand in the shoes of the righteous. By His grace, the gift of righteousness is credited onto our overdrawn accounts, and we can claim it for ourselves. "Though we may stand guilty before God" Chuck Swindoll writes, "we are *declared* just by means of a transfer of righteousness to our account from that of Jesus Christ."[64]

FAITH IS COUNTED AS RIGHTEOUSNESS

I would never call myself a great sportsman. In fact, I was never even that good an athlete, but I did manage to make the soccer team my junior year in college, and during that brief stint was the starting striker for the New Jersey Institute of Technology's soccer team.

To get that position I needed to prove myself. For starters, nearly a dozen other young men in their late teens to early twenties had vied for that coveted spot. I needed to ensure that I was in shape and had stamina and the skills to impress Coach Ricky Hill—outperform my peers to the degree that I would become the obvious choice.

A similar pattern follows every sport and nearly all other facets of human society. We insist on earning our own way. No sports team—from the neighborhood teams of wet-nosed five-year-olds to the musclemen of the NFL and the artist-like maneuvering of FIFA's stars—would ever select players who obviously lack the coordination and understanding of the game to contribute their fair share. We *must* earn our spots on the team. To make the cut, we have to prove ourselves capable—show we have what it takes to help the team win.

Fortunately, righteousness does not quite work this way. If righteousness were a sports team, no one would ever make the cut.

The Bible paints a bleak picture of humanity when it comes to making it on God's team. In his letter to the Romans, Paul paints with heavy brush the sad portrait of human depravity.

As Swindoll observes in *Insight on Romans*, in the first three chapters of the book, Paul lays bare the case against of all humanity. He begins with "the upright intellectual Gentile" in chapter one, proving that in spite of his scholarly flare and self-assessed wisdom, he is in fact a "simpering fool" who focuses all of his attention on the creation rather than the Creator.

In chapter two, Swindoll says, Paul moves on to "the self-satisfied crusader, the self-righteous moralist," who for his part thinks himself above reproach. Besides, he practices a punctilious conformity to the law, a mechanical compliance to the standards of righteousness it prescribes, and should therefore be deemed righteous before God. But Paul reveals that he, too, fails the test, for beneath his claims to righteousness beats a heart of corruption and degeneracy.

Then in chapter three Paul turns his attention to "his fellow sons of the covenant"—the Jewish nation. Chosen by God, and given

His precious Word, they prove to be as guilty as the rest, squandering their privileged state by their willful acts of disobedience. In the end they are deserving of God's wrath all the same.[65]

Finally, in Romans 3:10, Paul pronounces the verdict against the whole of humanity: there is none righteous, no, not one.

More than 7.4 billion souls inhabit planet earth.[*] Among them are missionaries, pastors, teachers, philanthropists, seminary professors, religious conference presidents, rabbis, self-proclaimed prophets, priests, cardinals, and even a pope. Yet not one human being, *no, not a single one*, can have the audacity to claim righteousness in his or her own merit.

You can turn to the patriarchs of yesteryears, go to the archives of the ages searching for history's most self-sacrificing, most honorable men and women. You will find some truly remarkable souls, people whose lives have had an incredible impact on this planet. You will discover the likes of Martin Luther, Mother Theresa, Martin Luther King Jr., Mohandas K. Gandhi, Ellen G. White, the apostles Paul, Peter and John, King David, the great scholar Moses, wise king Solomon, the prophets Samuel, Daniel, Isaiah, and Elisha, the preacher of righteousness Noah, the warriors Barack, Joshua, Caleb, and Gideon, strongman Samson, prayer warriors like Hannah and Hezekiah, God's companion Enoch, faithful servant Abel, and His first creature Adam.

In their rank are the best that humanity has to offer. Having searched their files and read the records they have set, you would be tempted to rise up and cheer, to applaud their patient endurance, their wisdom, power and pure human fortitudes.

But at the end of their performance evaluations, when compared to God's perfect standards, you would be forced to stamp in bold red letters atop each of their thick records: FAILURE! For

---

* As of June 2016

according to Paul, at the end of the righteousness tryout, God takes all of humanity and lumps every last one of our efforts into the same bucket: worthless.

There is no one who understands.

No one who seeks God.

All have turned away, they have together become worthless.

There is no one who does good, *not even one.*

God finds no one good enough to put on the roster sheet. No one makes the cut—not even one.

Making the Cut

Before you sit sullenly on the sideline, beating yourself up for not having tried hard enough or agonizing over the fact that you simply do not have what it takes to make God's righteousness team, I invite you to keep reading Romans 3. There is *one* way in which you can actually make the team. Here is Paul again:

"But now apart from the law the righteousness of God has been made known, to which the Law and the Prophets testify. This righteousness is given *through faith in Jesus Christ* to all who believe" (Romans 3:21, 22).

Your legs are too short, your reach too limited. Your aim is not good enough to hit the target. You do not have the strength or endurance to be successful on this team, and you certainly lack the skills to earn your way. Nevertheless God, the Coach, decides to put you on the starting lineup. In spite of your lack of coordination and obvious physical deficiencies, you still get a spot on the team.

The gospel is, indeed, good news!

Because human beings cannot in any way live up to God's righteousness requirements, He goes to their righteousness account books, overdrawn with a huge negative balance and no overdraft protection, and makes a deposit large enough to put them back in the black. This is the only way that anyone could ever be found righteous before God.

As you would expect, there *is* a catch: you must accept God's righteousness *by faith*. It is given with no reference to the bootstrap, self-help type promoted by the Jews of Jesus' day. Righteousness comes by faith; the only "fare" you pay for it is your belief in God. Abraham is the Bible's prime example of righteousness by faith.

When God found Abraham (Abram at the time), he was just one of many who bowed down in prayer to images of foreign gods carved out of wood and stone. Wanting to save the world from the same fate toward which Abraham was heading, God made a covenant with him.

"The Lord had said to Abram, 'Leave your country, your people and your father's household and go to the land I will show you. I will make you into a great nation and I will bless you; I will make your name great, and you will be a blessing. I will bless those who bless you, and whoever curses you I will curse; and all peoples on earth will be blessed through you'" (Genesis 12:1–3).

Abraham's response was immediate. He *obeyed* God by leaving behind his family and country for some unknown destination. He went on to win some great, decisive battles while losing others miserably. But after ten years of waiting and hoping, Abraham wondered if God really meant what He said. "'O Sovereign Lord, what can you give me since I remain childless and the one who will inherit my estate is Eliezer of Damascus?' And Abram said, 'You have given me no children; so a servant in my household will be my heir'" (Genesis 15:2, 3).

Abraham looked around and thought, "This isn't gonna work. Look at me! I'm eighty-five years old; my wife is in her mid-70s. We are literally as good as dead, and have no children. How can God say He will make me 'a great nation'? Is that even possible at my age?"

Abraham had crossed the thresholds of human possibilities. What he was promised simply could not happen in the natural world—not by a long shot. He was too old, his wife's body too advanced in years and not suited for child bearing. Everything around Abraham told him that what God promised could not happen on this side of eternity.

But because God said He would do it, even though his heart told him otherwise, even though everything he knew pointed to the contrary, "against all hope, Abraham in hope believed!" (Romans 4:18). This is what is meant by righteousness by faith. He trusted God's all-sufficiency to accomplish what was seemingly impossible, accepted God's word as sure and true, believed in His character, merit, and honor. He rose beyond his natural inclinations, beyond his circumstances, to believe in God's faithfulness.

"Without weakening in his faith, he faced the fact that his body was as good as dead—since he was about a hundred years old— and that Sarah's womb was also dead. *Yet he did not waver through unbelief regarding the promise of God, but was strengthened in his faith and gave glory to God, being fully persuaded that God had power to do what he had promised.* This is why 'it was credited to him as righteousness'" (Romans 4:19–22).

God responded to Abraham's faith by declaring him righteous. It was not because Abraham was beyond reproach or had somehow done enough good deeds to merit the designation. To the contrary, he was still a flawed man with a faltering, rickety faith (see Genesis 16:1–4; 17:15–18), a man who would continue to struggle with issues of doubt, who would continue to make mistakes and experience failures. But because he had faith, God took righteousness from His own account and made a balance transfer onto Abraham's, such that he could now be called righteous. Righteousness had nothing to do with Abraham's obedience or good deeds—it was a gift from God, granted the man simply because he believed.

Righteousness is not received because we go on a pilgrimage across the country on our knees, because we burn ourselves, or because we build hospitals for sick children. You can never pull yourself into righteousness with your own bootstraps; our very nature renders us unworthy. As Swindoll observes, it's not only because of what we *do*, but also because of what we *are*. You and I can never keep the law well enough to make ourselves worthy.

The only way for us to achieve righteousness is through the grace of God by faith in the merit of His Son Jesus Christ. Faith is what makes possible the balance transfer of righteousness from God's account to ours, but even having faith does not mean we suddenly qualify. Rather, faith becomes the *means* through which God applies *His* righteousness to us.

"Our only hope is to receive the righteousness of God as a gift by believing God's promise. Righteousness is really a five-letter word. You spell it F-A-I-T-H."[66]

LIFESTYLE OF THE JUST

WHEN it comes to serving justice, humanity's performance over the centuries leaves something to be desired. Our legal systems are flawed. A verdict of innocence (complete exoneration) or guilt (life sentence, execution, etc.) is not always based on whether or not a crime was committed. Sometimes it is your race, social standing, or financial situation. Acquittal can depend on how good your attorney is, how powerful you are, what neighborhood you live in, or whether or not you look guilty.

Yet even our faulty sense of justice sometimes cries foul when someone whom we know is obviously guilty escapes judgment. If men can detect a travesty of justice and call for the punishment of the guilty, how can God—who has a perfect sense of justice—actually *award* righteousness to murderers like King David, drunks like Noah, liars like Abraham, and temper-throwers like Moses? How can folks like you and me, caught with blood on our hands, receive the designation of "righteous"?

The answer comes down to a very important word: Justification.

Justification is a legal designation. Being justified means you have been vindicated, acquitted. When Paul says we "are justified freely by his grace" (Romans 3:24) he is saying that we have been made a declaration of right to righteousness. Righteousness has been decreed, ordained, authorized; we have been "endorsed" for it.

While justification happens instantly, it does not suddenly change your character. Your sin-diseased heart is still corrupt, and inside of you are found the same tendencies toward evil. The only difference heretofore is your standing before God. Rather than seeing you for who and what you truly are—a condemned convict on spiritual death row—God endorses you to be what Christ is: righteous.

"Justification is the sovereign act of God whereby He declares righteous the believing sinner—while he is still in a sinning state. Even though Abraham (after believing and being justified) would continue to sin from time to time, God heard Abraham when he said, "I believe... I believe in You." And God credited divine righteousness to his account. This occurred even though Abraham was still in a sinning state. But never again would the man have to worry about where he stood before his God. He was, once and for all, declared righteous."[67]

But since we continue to sin, how do we maintain our designation as "righteous"?

Excellent question. In his commentary on Paul's letter to the Romans, Charles Swindoll compares the difficult transition that the slaves had to make after their emancipation to the struggle of some Christians to break free from sin.

For most former slaves, slavery was all they knew. Although they hoped and prayed that the day would come when they would be free, freedom came at a price. They were now in charge of their own destinies, needed to provide for themselves and their children. The great questions of life—questions of citizenship, of a home and living, of education, the rearing of children, etc.—were thrown at them to answer for themselves, and many found these questions too overwhelming. So they reverted to slavery even though, legally, they had been free and no longer had any obligation to the "old master."

A great number of Christians, likewise, struggle to break free from the old master of sin. God has made the necessary provisions for our freedom. He paid the full penalty for our sins, offers us salvation at the cost of His own dear Son. But because it is difficult and unnatural for us humans to live free from sin, many Christians maintain their allegiance to it.[68]

Because we are justified by faith in Christ, our identities are aligned with His. Jesus died on the cross for our sins; we died *to* sin. He rose victoriously from the dead to a new life; we are called to live in newness of life. Since our identity is wrapped up in Christ, given that sin has no power over Him, we have received spiritual emancipation from sin as well. But you and I both know from the trenches that living a pure, holy, sinless life is a challenge that the best and brightest of God's heroes have struggled and still struggle to overcome. This brings us to another term: sanctification.

Sanctification (Greek, *hagiasmos*) means "consecration," "holiness." Things that are sanctified have been "made holy," "set apart" or "separated from common use." Sanctification is not like flipping on a light switch. It is a process of character development, of remaking us into Christ's image. Whereas justification happens instantly, sanctification takes a lifetime. We work hard at it, make the decision every day to be sanctified. Matthew Henry tells us that in order to attain sanctification we must go through these two phases: mortification and renewal.[69]

Mortification is death of self. It means we can no longer live in sin. We must make a constant effort to starve our sinful desires and tendencies until they become weak and eventually die. The former days when this old master used to command our attention by kindling a fire in our mortal bodies and use their members as its puppets to commit evil acts of unrighteousness are long gone. *Sin does not live here anymore,* the sign on our doorposts should read. The axe has been put to its roots; its throne is destroyed. A new throne has been erected in its stead, and a new master has the scepter: righteousness.

Renewal, for its part, means we now "live a new life" (Romans 6:4). This means we now walk to different beats, live by new sets of rules. Our lives are under new management, Swindoll says. We now live for God, and make deliberate efforts to surrender ourselves to Him in words and actions, to yield to Him in thoughts and aspirations, to seek His pleasure in recreation, employment, and in interaction with our family and friends. We employ our talents "in slavery to righteousness leading to holiness" (verse 19), meaning we engage ourselves in activities that promote God, forming habits of righteousness and growing in grace in the process.

The process of becoming a man or woman after God's own heart is a grueling, difficult journey where, moment by moment, we seek to mold our character after that of Christ. It requires prayer, reliance on God's Spirit, and deliberate efforts on our part—not wishful thinking or good intentions. But be warned—you are in for a hard fight, because the old master will not loosen its grip easily.

As it took months and countless lives following the emancipation

THE **AUDACITY** OF FAITH

declaration of September 1862 before all of the slaves would receive their freedom, your old master will not go down without a fight. He will swear and threaten and kick and scream. He will declare war on your life. And your penchant toward sin will entice you to head back to the field or to the big house, revel again with the old crowd, go back for a taste of the old wine.

Nevertheless you *must* stay the course, fight the good fight for righteousness' sake; do whatever it takes to rid your life of sin's influences. At the end of the battle, when you have reached the end of your faith, God in His grace will reward your efforts.

THE END OF OUR FAITH

COLLEGE has traditionally been viewed as the ticket to a better future. When I was growing up my mother Simone insisted that all of her kids get a college degree—no exception. As an immigrant who struggled to find jobs, she did not want us to have the same troubles. In fact, Mom has always been a big proponent of post-graduate education, to give us a competitive edge.

Whether you view college as surety for a good job or as a way to broaden and deepen your ability to think and act critically, the point is that college helps prepare you for tomorrow, to make you a better, more engaged citizen. It is foolish for anyone to think of college as only a place to have fun and meet people, play sports, party, and join fraternities or sororities. College is about the future, about what happens *after* you've received your degree and are deemed competent to enter "the real world."

For the Christian, life on earth is like being on a college campus. We are not here for the purpose of enjoying ourselves. This is a probationary period; we are here to prepare for glory. Now is a time during which we learn to be citizens of heaven, to prepare to enter the *real* real world.

Many insist on living their best life here on earth. They prefer a Christianity that ushers them to "live on top of the world," a gospel with no Cross, no suffering, no dying Savior. Their greatest concern is not some distant future reward. They want that too, but will worry about it when that distant future becomes the present. So they sacrifice the eternal for the temporal, forfeit their right to incredible riches in glory for all eternity, to pursue some tiny carrot dangled before their noses in the form of earthly power and riches.

A casual reading of Scripture shows that God's greatest concerns are not about how much money you have in the bank, how luxurious your home and ride are, how promising your career is, or how healthy you look and feel. Not that He is against those things, but God's greatest concern is the salvation of your soul, what becomes of you when the sun has set on your life, the trumpet has sounded, the great record books are opened, and you must now reap the harvest of how you lived on earth. His greatest concern is *your best life then*—your eternal destiny.

Some people go to college and concentrate on learning, doing their work, maturing, and finishing their studies on time or early. Others choose to enjoy the ride, spend their time carousing, and end up either squandering precious years or dropping out altogether. It is the same with this Christian life.

You can choose to make your time here a time of learning, growth, transformation, and preparation or you can become a complacent, mediocre Christian who spends his time pleasure-seeking and wealth-accumulating. The choice will determine whether you succeed or flunk. I hope, for your sake, that you live your best life now preparing for your best life *then*—spend time reading and studying God's Word, loving and helping your neighbor in need, and maturing through overcoming in times of trials. These pursuits, which characterized Christ's life, will revive and restore God's image in you and prepare you for eternity with Him and His holy angels.

Cashing Out

Every single human being lives his or her life toward one of two great destinations. "'When the Son of Man comes in his glory, and all the angels with him, he will sit on his throne in heavenly glory'" Jesus said. "'All the nations will be gathered before him, and he will separate the people one from another as a shepherd separates the sheep from the goats. He will put the sheep on his right and the goats on his left'" (Matthew 25:31–33).

One day God will call the world to judgment, and after reviewing the records of how we lived, He will separate us into two groups.

One group He will put on His right hand side, a place of honor. These are the folks who were not perfect, who struggled with sin and made mistakes like everybody else, but they loved Jesus, and tried their best to serve Him wholeheartedly. They had faith, believed in God when He made no sense, and held onto Him at all costs. They made conscious efforts each day to do what's right, not to receive a reward but because they loved Jesus and considered serving Him their greatest privilege in life. In the end God will declare them righteous and offer them a reward. It will not be what they had earned for themselves, but what Christ the Son of God had earned on their behalf.

The other group Christ will put on His left, a place of dishonor and contempt. These will be the naysayers, the skeptics, and those with blatant disregard for anything holy and sacred. It will also comprise those who were passive, who called themselves non-affiliates. God was ignored, His sacrifices viewed as foolishness, His commands as sadistic or selfish, His Word as fiction. He was not trusted, not respected, and was treated as inferior. Those among them who claimed to be "Christians" did not take God seriously enough to honor Him or obey His commands. They preferred to pursue their own agendas, revel in their sins, live with no restraint. College was a blast! Then came the final exam...and they flunked.

Since they rejected Christ's standards of righteousness—which He merited on their behalf through His sacrificial death—God will have no choice but to give them what *they* have earned for themselves. They will be found guilty and awarded eternal shame.

Wealthy parents, when they do their estate planning, often leave each of their children an inheritance. As anyone who is wealthy can attest, they must work hard not only to build their wealth but also to protect it. Dangers lurk at every turn for the wealthy: from crooks to thieves to fire to the government (taxes) to the economy to natural disasters to depreciation and degradation of assets. If the wealthy are not diligent they can easily lose their fortune.

The apostle Peter affirms that those whom Jesus declares "righteous" will also receive an inheritance. But this "inheritance [is] incorruptible" (1 Peter 1:4, NKJV). It "can never perish, spoil or fade" (NIV). It is not subject to decay, deterioration, or pollution. The government cannot tax you on it; the economy can't change your fortune and cause you to lose it; thieves cannot break in and steal it; fire cannot destroy it. Your inheritance is secure, backed by the guarantee of heaven's impenetrable vault. It is "kept in heaven for you" (1 Peter 1:4; see also Matthew 6:19, 20).

Paul tells us that this reward is so incredible the mind of man cannot conceive it. "'No eye has seen, no ear has heard, no mind has conceived what God has prepared for those who love him,'" he writes (1 Corinthians 2:9).

Our world is full of wonders. We have natural wonders like Mount Everest in Nepal, Victoria Falls in Zambia, and the Grand Canyon in the U.S. We also have engineering wonders, such as the Golden Gate Bridge in San Francisco, California, the Itaipu

Dam in Paraná, Brazil, the Forbidden City in Beijing, China, and the New Seven Wonders of the World. These show the beauty of our world and the genius of human engineering. Yet none of these beautiful structures and natural treasures can even begin to compare with what God prepares for those who serve Him faithfully.

The Bible mentions a city of which God Himself is the architect (see Revelation 21). It will be made of pure gold, and according to the Apostle John, it will shine "with the glory of God, and its brilliance was like that of a very precious jewel, like a jasper, clear as crystal" (Revelation 21:11). Can you imagine owning a house made of pure gold? The streets where you walk are of pure gold, the rocks on the street sides are like diamond?

God's City will have twelve gates each made with a single pearl. The walls will be of jasper, and it will have twelve foundations of the most precious stones. The water that flows in its river will be called "the water of life," and the City will have a tree whose leaves heal any and every possible disease you can imagine, causing everyone in it to live indefinitely—never once getting sick.

Some of you reading this may be thinking, *This is pure fiction!* I don't blame you. As Paul mentions above, the mind of man cannot conceive this truth. In fact, truth like this can only be accepted by faith, accepted simply because Jesus Christ, in His Word the Bible, says it is true.

In God's city words like AIDS, cancer, heart disease, and death will be forever banished from the dictionary. No more armed robberies, murders, prostitution, or fraud. No more acts of terrorism, no Al Qaeda, no planes crashing into towers, or bombings of buildings and train stations. There will be no more heartbreaking news of wars, no images of famished little children on the television set, no reporting of earthquakes and tsunamis and tornadoes that kill hundreds of thousands.

No one will have to worry about wrinkles or weight gain and ladies will not feel pressured to wear makeup to make them appear beautiful. There will be no need for crazy diets or liposuctions. We will all have incredible, beautiful, incorruptible bodies. No more tears, not even headaches, stomachaches, or the flu. God "'will wipe *every tear from their eyes,*'" John writes. "'There will be no more death or mourning or crying or pain, for the old order of things has passed away,'" (Revelation 21:4).

This is the reward that God promises to all who "make the cut." After years of disappointment and pain, we will finally receive the reward of our faith: eternal life. I don't know about you, but to me an eternity of lasting enjoyment and never-ending delight is worth the investment of seventy to ninety years of struggles on earth. Here is the apostle Peter again:

"In this you greatly rejoice, though now for a little while, if need be, you have been grieved by various trials, that the genuineness of your faith, *being* much more precious than gold that perishes, though it is tested by fire, may be found to praise, honor, and glory at the revelation of Jesus Christ, whom having not seen you love. Though now you do not see *Him,* yet believing, you rejoice with joy inexpressible and full of glory, receiving the end of your faith—the salvation of *your* souls" (1 Peter 1:6-9, NKJV).

Tickets Required

To get on a Greyhound bus and travel from Philadelphia, Pennsylvania to Orlando, Florida, you need a ticket. To take the Amtrak from Trenton, New Jersey to Boston, Massachusetts, you need a ticket. If you wish to board an airliner from John F. Kennedy airport in New York, USA to travel to Heathrow airport in London, England for a business trip then—*you guessed it!*—you need a ticket. Likewise, if you wish to travel from earth to glory, to vacation with Christ in heaven for 1,000 years, then return to live forever in God's new sparkling golden city on the earth restored to her pre-sin glory, you will most certainly need a ticket!

In the parable of the wedding banquet, recorded in Matthew 22:1–14, the Master's invited guests blew Him off and killed His servants. After dealing with the murderers, the Master extended the invitation to the wedding banquet to the world at large. People working in the fields, shopping at the marketplaces, those on the highways, at the offices, everyone everywhere was called to come celebrate with the Master and His Son, and a great number of guests came.

When the Host entered the banquet hall, He found a man who was not properly attired for this very special banquet. The condition for admission was clear. In order to enjoy the festivities, the guests needed to wear a special, very costly robe that the King Himself had prepared. Knowing the invitation was sudden and unexpected, and that nothing the guests had in their closets would be "good enough," the King provided the wedding apparel, which each guest was to pick up at the door and change into *before* entering the banquet hall.

The idea was that when the King walked into the banquet hall, He would be honored to see all of the guests appropriately dressed. Perhaps the raiment would coordinate with the decorations; perhaps it was simply a matter of personal taste. What's important is that it was *His* banquet, and as such He had the right to set the expectations. Anyone who refused to wear the garment provided could simply turn around and leave without entering the hall.

When the King noticed one guest clothed in his own off-color, unmatched, uncoordinated apparel, which by the way must have stuck out like a sore thumb, He was understandably irritated. He challenged the nonconforming guest, wondering how he even made it into the hall wearing *that.*

The man was speechless. It's not that he was unaware of the requirements—he had been made aware; it's not as though no clothing had been made available to him—one was provided. But for whatever reason he decided that what he had on was good enough. While he wanted to partake fully of the King's bounties, he did not honor or respect Him enough to comply with the rules.

Because of the man's wrong choice he was to be thrown out. "' "Tie him hand and foot," '" the King ordered, "' "and throw him outside, into the darkness, where there will be weeping and gnashing of teeth" '" (Matthew 24:13).

The apostle Peter writes, "But in keeping with his promise we are looking forward to *a new heaven and a new earth, where righteousness dwells*" (2 Peter 3:13). God's new heaven and earth are home to righteousness. You cannot enter His new city, let alone dwell there, unless you are righteous.

It's like trying to enter the concert hall to see your favorite artist or the theater to view a long-awaited performance. You're at the door, eager to enter, and can't wait to get in. But you haven't got a ticket. You need one to get in and enjoy the show. Nothing else will do, because the mean-looking, tough-as-nails ticket collector won't even allow a peek inside unless you produce that coveted ticket.

This is tough news for us earthlings because, as we mentioned earlier, *no one* is righteous, no, not one! Fortunately, Christ made *all* of the provisions necessary for us to get into the venue. Our own personal designer robe, tailored to our size, is pressed and waiting for us at the door to the banquet hall. Our ticket is available at will call; all we need to do is pick it up! I'm so excited to write this! The word that comes to mind is, *glory!*

But don't make the foolish mistake of thinking you can just waltz over and grab a ticket. You are still expected to meet certain obligations.

"Wait a minute!" you may protest. "I thought you said the ticket was *free!* What do you mean by 'obligations'?"

Yes, the tickets *are* free, and yes, the Coach *will* give you a spot on the righteousness team even though you are not "good enough." Nevertheless you cannot make it on the team if you simply stay home watching reality TV. At a minimum you must show up at practice; you must come to tryout. So while nothing you have can compensate the King for the ticket, He still requires a small donation, one proportional to the size of your bank account. There is a fare, so to speak: and the fare is *faith!*

Whether you are poor, wealthy, or in the "middle class," you will pay a fare. Don't worry, it won't be too exorbitant. You can certainly afford to pay it. But make no mistake—righteousness comes at some personal cost; it requires faith—battle-tested, forged-in-the-trenches, raw-deal faith.

The good news is no matter how much faith we have—grand like the great Moses who saw God's back; enduring like giant of faith Job who said, "Though he slay me, yet will I hope in him!" or like the rickety, wobbly faith of the desperate father who cried, "'I do believe; help me overcome my unbelief!'"—if our faith is genuine, God will honor it, and by His grace grant us righteousness.

I will say it again, *glory!*

All Are Invited
The Matthew 22:1–14 parable is symbolic of the great feast of the ages, and God is the Host. He invites all of the righteous to celebrate with Him the end of sin and the beginning of the reign of righteousness. The book of Revelation dubs this the marriage celebration between Jesus Christ and His bride, the church. "'For the marriage of the Lamb has come, and His wife has made herself ready'" the apostle John heard a great multitude shout (Revelation 19:7, NKJV).

And guess what? *You're invited!*

God calls the whole world to come party with Him. He offers

the rewards of righteousness to every single human being. No matter what nation you hail from, what your race or your financial situation is; no matter what you do for a living, your social standing or how old you are, God calls all to feast on His lavish bounties—no one is excluded.

"'Come, all you who are thirsty, come to the waters; and you who have no money, come, buy and eat! Come, buy wine and milk without money and without cost'" (Isaiah 55:1).

God calls the heads of state of the most powerful nations in the world, "Come!"

He calls the billionaires and millionaires of planet earth, "Come!"

He calls the unemployed, "Come!"

He calls those who now labor for minimum wages, "Come!"

To the beggar by the street side He says, "Come!"

The ones who auction their lives away for cheap hear the same invitation, "Come!"

The preacher hears Him say, "Come!"

The same word echoes to the prostitute in the rundown motel room, "Come!"

To the murderer, the homosexual, the liar, the wife-beater, the sex addict, the tax evader, the porn watcher, and to the fraud He makes the same invitation, "'Come to me, all you who are weary and burdened, and I will give you rest'" (Matthew 11:28).

Not all will accept the invitation, but everyone is invited. And only those who are properly attired will get to stay in the banquet hall to enjoy the festivities. Whether or not they understanding why the costly festal garment is given, they *must* put it on.

As you may have guessed by now, the garment is a symbol of Christ's righteousness. In Revelation it is presented as a long white robe, bright and clean; the color white symbolizes purity and holiness. The bride—God's church—must wear the robe of Christ's purity and holiness to participate in this great banquet (Revelation 19:8; 7:9-14). No one can stay in the banquet hall without it. For a time you may fool all of the other guests into believing that you belong. You may even convince the servants at the door that you've made the cut. But sooner or later, when the Host arrives, He will detect right away who is and who isn't properly attired, and all offending parties will be packed up, tied up, and thrown outside where they belong.

My prayer is for you to have faith the righteousness that comes by faith. When He returns you, I, and everyone who lived by faith, will see Him come in the clouds of heaven. Instead of running away to hide in caves and under rocks, we will say with the redeemed of all ages and times, "'Behold, this *is* our God; we have waited for Him, and He will save us. This *is* the Lord; we have waited for Him; we will be glad and rejoice in His salvation'" (Isaiah 25:9, NKJV).

LAST WORDS
Faith Matters

WHY does faith matter?

The word "faith" appears 242 times in the King James Bible. Obviously it is not as popular as words like "father," which appears 974 times, or "spirit" (501 times), or the Bible's two most popular nouns, which is fitting: "Lord" (7,365 times) and God (4,293 times).* Nevertheless, above and beyond most other more popular terms, faith matters.

Faith matters because it is critical to our existence. Without faith you will not put on a pair of pants, fly in an airplane, or sit in your dentist's chair.

More than this, faith matters because it transforms. It turns hard-as-stone hearts into breeding grounds for God's grace, transforms

---

* See www.kingjamesbibleonline.org

former murderers into preachers and prophets, prostitutes into virtuous servants.

Faith matters because it is essential. It is the most vital ingredient of the Christian experience. Without faith salvation is a joke, and the Bible is fiction. Without it we stumble through life aimlessly until we wither and die.

Faith matters because it is the most powerful force in the cosmos. It bridges the gulf between impossibility and reality, gives us access to the limitless powers of Almighty God. It leads to a defiant audacity that empowers mere humans to move the God of the universe, and stamps upon us the character of Jesus Christ.

Lastly, faith matters because it is the secret to pleasing God. It is the fare one must possess to attain righteousness, which is the key that unlocks the vault of heaven. Without faith there is no righteousness, no heaven, no afterlife, no salvation. Death becomes the great victor, and our lives mere instants in time—where we live a few decades, die, then disappear into the archives of history. We need faith to receive grace, faith to see the face of Jesus, faith to live beyond our earthly years and access eternity.

Beyond treasures, beyond riches and honor, invest your time building your faith in God. Even if it cost you everything—family, friends, health and safety, your very life—get faith. Why? Because when you have faith, you have everything. If your life on earth would matter, you need faith. Faith is worth it. Faith matters.

Get faith!

ENDNOTES

CHAPTER ONE
THE POWER TO SWING GOD'S ARMS

1. Philip Yancey, *Reaching for the Invisible God* (Grand Rapids, MI: Zondervan, 2000), p 47
2. Craig Groeschel, *Weird* (Grand Rapids, MI: Zondervan, 2011), p 20
3. Roy Adams, *Crossing Jordan: Joshua, the Holy War, and God's Unfailing Promises* (Hagerstown, MD: Review and Herald Publishing Association, 2004), p 107
4. Ibid., p 116
5. James Montgomery Boice, *Joshua* (Grand Rapids, MI: Baker Books, 1989), p 80
6. Ibid., p 80

CHAPTER TWO
REACHING WITH A PURPOSE

7. Lamb, Robert, and Michael Morrissey. "How Bridges Work" 01 April 2000. HowStuffWorks.com. <http://science.howstuffworks.com/engineering/civil/bridge.htm> 16 September 2012
8. Philip Yancey, *Disappointment with God* (Grand Rapids, MI: Zondervan, 1988), pp 137, 138
9. Philip Yancey, *Reaching for the Invisible God* (Grand Rapids, MI: Zondervan, 2000), pp 135, 136
10. Os Guinness, *The Call* (Nashville, TN: W Publishing, 1998, 2003), p 65
11. Philip Yancey, *Disappointment with God*, p 230
12. Ibid., p 228
13. Ibid., p 52
14. Ibid., p 53

CHAPTER THREE
DIVINE INCONVENIENCE

15. Doug Bachelor, *At Jesus' Feet* (Hagerstown, MD: Review and Herald Publishing Association, 2001), pp. 184, 185.
16. E. G. White, *Patriarchs and Prophets* (Washington, DC: Review and Herald Publishing Association, 1958), p 248
17. Charles Swindoll, Moses: *A Man of Selfless Dedication* (Nashville: Word Publishing, 1999), p 79
18. Philip Yancey, *Disappointment with God* (Grand Rapids, MI: Zondervan, 1988), p 233
19. E. G. White, *The Desire of Ages* (Mountain View, CA: Pacific Press Publishing Association, 1898, 1940) p 19
20. Revised and edited by Francis Nathan Peloubet and Mary Abby Thaxter Peloubet, Smith Bible Dictionary (Nashville, TN: Thomas Nelson Publishers, 1986), p 383
21. White, *The Desire of Ages,* p 145
22. As quoted by Doug Bachelor, p 185

CHAPTER FOUR
GOD'S 20/20

23. Carl Bianco, MD, "How Vision Works." April 1, 2000. www.HowStuffWorks.com. <http://science.howstuffworks.com/life/human-biology/eye1.htm > March 26, 2013
24. Philip Yancey, *Reaching for the Invisible God* (Grand Rapids, MI: Zondervan, 2000), p 69
25. Bennie R. Crockett Jr., *Prisons of the First Century,* Biblical Illustrator, 31/4 (Summer 2005), p 46-49
26. Edited by Martin H. Manser, *The New Matthew Henry Commentary* (Grand Rapids, MI: Zondervan, 2010), p 1947
27. E. G. White, *The Acts of the Apostles* (Mountain View, CA: Pacific Press Publishing Association, 1911), p 214
28. White, p 215
29. White, p 217

CHAPTER FIVE
MUSTARD SEED EFFECT

30. Philip Yancey, *Disappointment with God* (Grand Rapids, MI: Zondervan, 1982), p 155, 161

31. Philip Yancey, *What's So Amazing About Grace?* (Grand Rapids, MI: Zondervan, 1997), p 11
32. Os Guinness, *The Call: Finding and Fulfilling the Central Purpose of Your Life* (Nashville, TN: W Publishing, 2003) p 59
33. Charles R. Swindoll, *Insights on Romans* (Grand Rapids, MI: Zondervan, 2010), p 323
34. Charles R. Swindoll, *Moses: A Man of Selfless Dedication* (Nashville, TN: Word Publishing, 1999), p 193
35. Guinness, p 65
36. Charles R. Swindoll, *Moses: A Man of Selfless Dedication*, p 206

CHAPTER SIX
THE SCANDAL OF GRACE

37. Max Lucado, *Grace* (Nashville, TN: Thomas Nelson, 2012), p 36
38. Philip Yancey, *The Jesus I Never Knew* (Grand Rapids, MI: Zondervan, 1995) p 144
39. Charles R. Swindoll, *The Grace Awakening* (Nashville, TN: Thomas Nelson, 2003), p 23
40. Lucado, pp 19, 21
41. Philip Yancey, *What Good Is God?* (New York, NY: Faith Works, 2010), p 244
42. Max Lucado, *Grace* (Nashville, TN: Thomas Nelson, 2012), p 10
43. Yancey, *What Good Is God?*, p 282
44. Charles R. Swindoll, *Insights on Romans* (Grand Rapids, MI: Zondervan, 2010), p 243
45. Swindoll, *The Grace Awakening*, p 2
46. E. G. White, *The Desire of Ages* (Mountain View, CA: Pacific Press Publishing Association, 1898, 1940) p 461
47. Insight for Living, God's Master Work, Vol. 3 (Job-Daniel), *Isaiah: Prince among the Prophets.* Air date: September 7, 2011
48. Philip Yancey, *What's So Amazing About Grace?* (Grand Rapids, MI: Zondervan, 1997), p 102, 103
49. Swindoll, *The Grace Awakening*, pp 134, 135
50. Doug Bachelor, *At Jesus' Feet* (Hagerstown, MD: Review and Herald Publishing Association, 2001), pp 21, 22
51. White, *The Desire of Ages*, p 741
52. White, *The Desire of Ages*, p 790

CHAPTER SEVEN
GIANTS OF OUR LIVES

53. Craig Groeschel, *Weird* (Grand Rapids, MI: Zondervan, 2011), p 140
54. Os Guinness, *The Call: Finding and Fulfilling the Central Purpose of Your Life* (Nashville, TN: W Publishing, 2003), p 79
55. Roy Adams, *Crossing Jordan: Joshua, Holy War, and God's Unfailing Promises* (Hagerstown: Review and Herald Publishing Association, 2004), p 174
56. As quoted by James Montgomery Boice in *Joshua* (Grand Rapids, MI: Baker Books, 1980), p 103
57. Ibid., p 104

CHAPTER EIGHT
GOD PLACED A BET

58. Charles R. Swindoll, *Insights on James, 1 and 2 Peter* (Grand Rapids, MI: Zondervan, 2010), p 155
59. Philip Yancey, *Disappointment with God* (Grand Rapids, MI: Zondervan, 1988), p 188
60. Charles R. Swindoll, *Job: A Man of Heroic Endurance* (Nashville, TN: Thomas Nelson, Inc., 2004), p 33
61. C.S. Lewis, *A Grief Observed* (New York: HarperOne, 1964), pp 5, 6
62. Charles R. Swindoll, *David: A Man of Passion and Destiny* (Nashville, TN: Thomas Nelson, Inc., 2000), p 120
63. Philip Yancey, *Disappointment with God* (Grand Rapids, MI: Zondervan, 1982), p 284

CHAPTER NINE
THE END OF OUR FAITH

64. Charles R. Swindoll, *Insights on Romans* (Grand Rapids, MI: Zondervan, 2010), p 83
65. Ibid, pp 65, 66
66. Ibid, p 99
67. Charles R. Swindoll, *The Grace Awakening* (Nashville, TN: Thomas Nelson, 2003), p 21
68. Swindoll, *Insights on Romans* p128
69. Edited and updated by Martin H. Manser, *The New Matthew Henry Commentary* (Grand Rapids, MI: Zondervan, 2010), pp 2022, 2023

CPSIA information can be obtained
at www.ICGtesting.com
Printed in the USA
BVOW06*2133230217
476693BV00003B/5/P